Mary Magdalene:
A Historic Novel

Sandra Cerda

This Novel is part of
The Mary Magdalene Collection:
*Film - Book - Study Guide - Journal - Products & More
See, www.MaryMagdalene.Film for details*

New Life Publishing
Bringing *1ˢᵗ Time Authors* to Print!

On Facebook @ *1ˢᵗ Time Authors.*

For life & love
in and through Jesus Christ
and all who *cannot rest*
until they find it.

A very special heartfelt *love and appreciation* to all who supported me with prayer and guidance throughout the process of writing and creating, developing, and producing the story of Mary Magdalene, *to the Glory of God.*

...and to my family.

For my children and theirs to a thousand generations, *Jesus is Lord!*

CONTENTS

*"Woman, where are your accusers,
has no one condemned you?"*

"No one Lord."

"Neither do I condemn you,
go and *sin no more."*

John 8:11

Mary Magdalene

The grief of this woman,
whose life was changed by her
personal encounter with Jesus,
is the grief of us all, in our darkest moments.

Pope Francis

on Mary Magdalene

For centuries
Mary Magdalene has been portrayed as a
repentant prostitute who became physically & sexually involved
with our Lord and Savior Jesus Christ, although nothing in
the Gospels supports those claims. Not until the fourth century was
Mary called the "Apostle to the Apostles" by Orthodox
theologian Augustine. One of the most significant, intriguing,
and mysterious figures in Christianity, Mary was part of
a movement that transformed the world.
First to receive the mantle of Evangelism in the
New Testament, preaching the witnessed Resurrection of our
Lord Jesus, Mary would face fierce & fiery persecution for her
stalwart, unflinching faith in Him whom she loved.
With lifelong devotion, her story continues to reveal the power of
unconditional love and forgiveness, redemption, restoration, and
renewing of purpose in life, for even the least among us.
Freed of seven demons, her life's story continues to stir debate
among the elitist of scholars worldwide.
While some would stone her still, Mary Magdalene is held
in the Holy esteem of sainthood by the Catholic, Orthodox,
Anglican, and Lutheran churches
and most of the world.

During the time of the Slaughter of Innocents
Jesus was taken from Bethlehem as a child by his parents
into Egypt, as Herod the Great decreed:

All males aged two and younger
are ordered killed by the sword.

It was nearest the year, 3 A.D., and hundreds of babies
would be slain. Not far from Bethlehem in Magdal,
word arrived of the slaughter, as a young Mary learned
of the horrors of Herod, unaware life would one day lead her
to the very feet of Him, who would enrage the king's son,
the feet of God's mercy, Jesus.
The culture of her day had never made room for women,
and so, ruled by fears of religious laws as well as
those enforced by locals, the story of
Mary Magdalene
begins.

MARY

Red with blood, strewn dead bodies, fires burning along the shore. Many floated dead in the sea. Mary, *the Magdalene*, ran, jumping over the bodies of the dead. Thousands lay slain as a fleet of Romans rushed groups of Jews into the Galilee. Terrorized women and children fled, villagers and zealots fought hard against the onslaught of the raging annihilation of those who loved and believed in Jesus.

Crowds of the beaten and bleeding ran forced into the overcrowded boats that remained. Many elderly fought hard against the fray as guards pushed them hatefully into the bloody waters, drowning too many to count. Chaotic crowds frenzied through the floating dead; many were children.

Storm-tossed, the disheveled and bleeding survivors, Martha and Lazarus among them, arrived at the shore with Mary, their sister. Devastated by what they saw, they found the slaughter worse than they first feared. So many women and children lay dying or dead.

The sands of the shore stretched as far as the eye could see, red with blood. There was no place to run to, but the water.

Maximin and Sidonius, of the seventy evangelists, fought back hard, breaking through for the others. Sarah, Mary's servant, and Salome, *John and James' mother* struggled to catch up to the group.

Then the terrified crowd stampeded in terror, forcing many into the angry sea.

Lazarus struggled with his shackled ankle through knee-deep water to a small boat, grabbing it. "Over here! Maximin, help me!" cried Lazarus over the horrified crowd. Maximin hurried through to help. Sidonius arrived to help the men flip the boat. It was so heavy.

Sarah and Salome were being pulled by the tide. Frantically, they boarded with Sidonius' help.

Mary tried to reach her sister, who fought to stay above water.

Her bruised wrist shackled and her scratched face, bloody and bruised, Mary screamed, "Lazarus! Help me! Martha is drowning!" running toward her sister.

Martha could hardly stand when her terrified screams shrieked aloud, "Help me!" The waves swallowed her gurgling panic.

Reaching Martha before the waves could pull her under, Mary waded through the bodies of the lifeless, when her own feet lost their footing. "Lazarus!" she tried in vain to scream just as her head went under. Lazarus found and grabbed Mary's hair under the waves, pulling her up. Choking, she grabbed his face, screaming, "Jesus!" Seeing Lazarus, she turned and boarded the boat.

Lazarus and Sidonius lifted and pushed Martha into the boat over the distraught women, who huddled together soaked, cold, and shivering. Seeing the broken shackle on Martha's foot, Salome reached to help stop the bleeding. The men hurried to board as their feet had lost their firm stand to sinking sand beneath the raging waves.

Terrified, they clung to each other, Martha, and Salome sobbing in disbelief.

"Hurry! Harder! Row harder! Sarah!" yelled Mary over the deafening, terrified screams of the people. The frightened rowed hard as fast as they could. The shore faded.

The soul-piercing screams of the dying rose to the heavens, the slaughter in the distance roared as black smoke rose to a blue sky. The entire shore of the Galilee was ablaze. Over forty thousand slain. Many sold, many scattered. Many were children.

Adrift, the oar-less boat, loaded over with exhausted, sleeping survivors floated. Mary and Maximin, awake from the shock, searched every direction; there was no land in sight. Facing each other, the two could hear only the waves while they watched a burnt-red sunset fade to black.

Banking near the shore, the wearied group helped each other disembark. Half-dried, thin, and parched, they faced the new land.

"How long have we been lost?" Martha asked, falling to her knees, with her worn face toward the wet sand and her fingers dug into the grit.

Mary looked ahead, taking a deep breath. "Where are we?" she whispered just under her breath. Guided by the Spirit of the Lord, they had arrived near Gaul, Massilia.

"Thank you, Lord," whispered Martha, hoarsely.

A strained Maximin scanned the desolate shore. "Jesus said, 'go into all the world'... we are surely in the world now!" he pointed out, overwhelmed.

"But we are not *of* the world," reminded Mary quickly.

Martha sat on the sand looking ahead to the tree line, calling out, "'Lay hands on the sick' He also said." Sidonius reached to help her up.

"And cast out the devils!" chimed Salome.

"So, we go; preach all we know!" proclaimed Mary loudly.

"We preach?" Martha blurted turning her whole body toward Mary.

"Yes!" said Lazarus. "And raise the dead!"

Approaching Mary from behind, Sarah strained to see further inland, asking, "Where are we, Mary?" Peering ahead, trying to see past the shadowy trees, Sarah's damp skin bristled with fear. "Is that movement?" she asked, pointing toward the tree line, trying to make out what moved in the distance. One by one her eyes focused: natives emerged, then more. In a moment, the entire tree line revealed hundreds of men and boys holding weapons of war, their painted faces intimidating and fearful. Not willing to move an inch, Sarah held her breath.

Seeing what she pointed to, just as one native raised his spear, Mary warned in a whisper, "*Far* from home."

THE FORTRESS of MAGDALA

Early A.D.

30 YEARS EARLIER

Of noble birth, and that of royalty, Mary, the daughter of Cyrus and Eucharia of Magdala, a village on the shore of Galilee, lived near the sea. Along with her brother Lazarus, and sister Martha, they owned the Castle Magdalum and Bethany, as well as part of the city of Jerusalem.

The hopelessness of Mary's culture for women and children was all around, which echoed sounds of stress and troubled times. The faint cries of infants and loud verbal commands came almost as early as the cock's crow. This day was special for Mary, though.

It was early morning and a group walk through the countryside was the planned day's event as pilgrims journeyed to visit the graves of their deceased. Mary's family would join them to visit the grave of their mother, Eucharia. With her father weakened and aged, he would stay behind.

The rain had hardly cleared when it was time to start cleaning the *muddy splash and puddles* left behind. Elders would journey to the grave plots shortly. Mary *plunged through* painful memories of her mother's sudden death years earlier; now, she was only 12 years old.

A difficult age for young girls, even more so without her mother. It was the age acceptable for marriage, according to the customs of their faith. But these thoughts were far from Mary's innocent mind and heart.

She was lovely and kind. A thin braid rested on her shoulder on most days. Her gentle mannerisms and keen perception both complimented her beauty, in that she cared greatly for children and elders. Even with her gentle traits, Mary was also growing more resistant to the rigid customs and traditions held by her older siblings.

Peering through the thatched window with a mop rag in her hands, she wiped the spills and splashes that had made their way in.

5

Something between the cracks grabbed her attention: a small bird just outside her window had fallen from its nest, not yet able to fly. Peeking through the crack, she noticed broken eggshells near the frightened hatchling.

"Probably from the force of the winds," Mary whispered. Rushing, she tried not to draw attention from her sister, who ranted about the frivolous things Mary filled her time with. Gently, she recovered the hatchling, quickly finding solace in this tiny new life.

Carefully, scooping up the small bird into her cupped hands, Mary chuckled, "You're a dove-ling!" Excited, she discreetly retreated indoors hiding her discovery behind her. "You deserve a chance at a new life," she continued speaking to the tiny bird. Darting toward her sleeping cushions, she pulled out from under her pillows a small wooden box container. Aged and scratched but polished and clean, she emptied it of its contents: mostly dried flowers, river stones, and beads. Mary cradled the tiny bird. Tucking it along with the eggshells and grass she had brought along she made its new home. Proceeding to gather a few pieces of trim and things, Mary created a nest as Martha burst into the room unexpectedly early and loud.

"Quickly! Put those things away and gather your belongings! The day will be long enough. We depart soon!" yelled Martha, rushing through. Mary carefully scooted the hatchling back, hiding it discreetly.

"But we're only going past the ravine. Lazarus said we may camp near the swimming hole!" replied Mary, picking up her pace and aiding her sister.

"Lazarus only wants to swim, eat, and sleep. You do well to stay alert to what father needs. Now, go!" Rushing Mary out the door ahead of her, Martha glanced once more ensuring nothing stayed behind, grabbed a head covering, and left to join the caravan.

The pilgrims, although chiming a heart-felt solemn song, began a much livelier one: that of the fullness of life lived and the soon coming promised Messiah. Villagers joyfully sang beautiful, traditional hymns of times past. They made their way through winding paths, singing to help pass the time on an otherwise heavyhearted day.

Seeing Lazarus, Mary called, "Will we be camping out, brother? There's the wonderful swimming hole you spoke of?" hoping he would say yes.

"Not this trip, girl. Father is not well. We must return before dark. Get back with the older women now or Martha will come fetch you!" he scolded.

Ignoring him, Mary confided, "I noticed father paused more than usual. Perhaps he remembers mother more, today. Another time?" she hollered back, catching up to Martha.

"Where have you been this time, sister? Must I remain concerned for you? **Keep over here** with the women. Do yourself some good by it," warned Martha. "And cover your head!" she said tossing the lovely head-wrap to the girl. "You know better, Mary, do as you're told!"

"Talking with Lazarus," she replied panting and rushed. "We return before dark. He said father's not well."

"Yes, I noticed before anyone woke. I heard him wince in pain. We must help him more and pray, Mary," Martha responded.

Mary lessened her pace, seizing the chance to slip away. Unaware her servant-girl, Sarah, overheard them and already knew of Cyrus's worsening health, Mary whispered sadly, "My father loves me and would never leave me," fearful of losing him as well.

"I love you too, Mary," Sarah laughed mischievously, startling her.

"Little girl, I've known you forever!" hollered Mary. "You know I love you more!" Racing and chasing each other, they veered toward the grassy hillslope with all the other children spotting their destination ahead.

Martha continued to share her concerns for her heavyhearted father with the older women when she noticed Lazarus approached by villagers on horses. His face turning grievous at the news of Bethlehem, Lazarus wept at the decree of Herod. "It is a bloodbath, sir," cried the villager dismounting his exhausted horse. "So many died trying to save the children. All have run to the caves. The women wail to no end. Lazarus, there was no mercy!"

"These were thrust through!" shouted another rider angrily. "Trampled under horses, babes in arms. Hundreds lay slain trying to save them."

Horrified, Lazarus saw Martha who had fallen behind the others, waiting for him with concern. Reaching her, he shared the report as a shocked Martha fell in the arms of her brother at the news, "Why!" she screamed. Stunned at the wail echoing through the valley, Mary and others rushed back to see Martha now travailing on her knees.

"Herod! Like a thief in the night!" wept Lazarus aloud, unable to hold back his rage. "Vengeance is our God's! May our promised Deliverer come quickly!" he cried. "May our Deliverer vindicate our people of this slaughter, this massacre of innocent ones. These are blood-thirsty men," he wailed angrily, his voice echoing through the valley. The pilgrims gathered, grieving, mourning the deaths of so many.

Herod's decree to slaughter innocent infants was his enraged reaction toward the outwitting Magi. Herod sent out orders to put to death all boys two years and younger from Bethlehem to its surrounding vicinities. An Angel of the Lord warned Joseph, though, who took Mary and the infant Jesus, and escaped to Egypt. With this bloodshed of the innocent, Herod fulfilled the words of the prophet Jeremiah, *"A voice is heard in Rama, weeping and great mourning. Rachel weeping for her children and refusing comfort because they are no more.*" [1]

The people of the region never recovered from the tragic plunder of children. No one would ever forget the rage of Herod the Great, nor realize how long and far-reaching his dynasty would ruthlessly reign. One day, Mary would put the pieces together. Herod the Great was the king of the Jews[2], by Rome's order. Mary would learn, God had a different order. Over the years, the strain of loneliness in not having her mother opened the door to youthful pride and arrogance.

She grew resistant to the seriousness of her culture, especially regarding women. It was overbearing and suppressive, even "stripping" at times, she would complain in vain. In a short while, Mary would be a rumored rebel lacking obedience. Others would claim she was uncontrollable or unruly for her increasing challenges to authority, namely her siblings. Mary had grown rebelliously independent and worldly, as vanity made its way to her heart.

Her hair, long and lovely, as it was of all the women in her day, was customarily worn down loosely by married women or those of noble birth.

Although noble, Martha did not regard her sister's frivolous liberties very well. She preferred her younger sister upheld the more traditional customs. It was expected of all women of their faith.

Mary preferred to follow her own heart and express herself more freely, opening herself up more to the world. Courting discretion loosely, her naivety, mixed with her wild heart, would be an open invitation for indulgence and vanity whose curse would follow her the rest of her life.

---

[1] Jeremiah 31:15 and Matthew 2:18
[2] Bibleoddysey.org/herod-the-great

9

MAGDALA

Over 25 years had passed, their father long gone. Mary lessened her devotion to the things in life that made for peace and began to carve her own path.

The port-city of Magdala had grown in wicked lawlessness. Known by the less-than-merciful Romans of the day as a city of great sin in the region, the beautiful bordering coast of the Galilee masked the secret sins of those enslaved within. The success of Pilate's rival, the extravagant Port of Tiberius, would prove to be the start of Magdala's moral decline.

Ships from afar brought treasures, foods, and spices, wares such as precious stones of alabaster and treasures from throughout the Mediterranean region. Oils and salts for healing balms and medicines, henna and purple dyes used in celebrations, along with other rare items that were sought after, and so needed in the region.

Mary loved the sound and liveliness of the port where she was well-known for her own medicinal blends and business dealings, and for who she was: her father's daughter.

The Tower, as Magdala was known as, produced her salted fish for trade throughout the region and beyond. Like any other port of the day it too had few boundaries. Makeshift shanties, where villagers and merchants sold and traded their goods, lined the walkway to the piers. Some called those shanties home. It was a world all their own, overcrowded with a beautiful mix of cultures. With soldiers, peddlers, and merchants, even the homeless and forgotten called the port home. The vilest of the region found a place to hide there. Sin was rampant and restraint far from the minds of port dwellers as the smell of the world rested on the people.

There weren't many rules to follow at the port. Love was often traded for small hints of kindness, even if pretentious or vain. It mattered not to some. Others would coquet with and embrace perversions of immorality and debauchery, wickedness in the sight of the Lord, not far from the ways of Sodom or Gomorrah. Magdala was a vile place.

The corruption of ruling Rome made its way throughout the region with all its compromise, vanity, and sin. It was the sound of the world, the sound of the money changers. It was the sound of need, greed, and a covetous lust for more.

Beautiful ships passed through from Capernaum to Magdala to the ports of Tiberius and Jerusalem. These same ships took loved ones to the farthest corners of the world, many of whom often *never* returned.

It was not long before vanity and weary emptiness made their home in Mary's bitterly hardening heart. Soon she would yield to a life of hopeless despair with only a dimming, flickering ray of hope. Mary was lonely.

At her father's passing, she and her siblings inherited the great wealth of their father. Being more indulgent in the vanity of her youth than her sibling, her heart hardened as she busied herself with the things of the world. The young Mary used her beauty and wealth to fulfill her empty self with nothing but the desire of her heart and cravings of her flesh. She grew accustomed to this shadowy curse that accompanied her every move. It had long refused to loosen its grip off her mind, soul, and body.

Mary had lost her way in life, and with it her good name. Her rebellious nature and arrogance earned her a new name, "the sinner."

In a time when women had no value or voice, no sound worthy of being heard, and no way of inheritance, Mary held on to the blessing of her father. Yet even with that, she was well past the time of marriage for a girl in her world. Most were wed and having children before they turned sixteen. She though, along with her sister, would remain under the authority and covering of their brother, Lazarus, for they had no man in marriage. It was the law of the land. It was the law of their faith.

Now knighted, Lazarus was away for long, leaving the management of the estate to Martha, the older, more prudent and responsible of the three. Martha cared for the multiple servants and countless poor who came daily for help. With Lazarus away so often and

Martha consumed by the time and attention to the estate and the people in her care, Mary busied herself with trying to make up the difference and for lost time.

It would fall to Mary to make the trips to the port and deal with merchants more often than she cared for. Traders, relentless in their pursuit of her, made her responsibilities much harder to bear. Her reputation for being her father's daughter would go before her as well as her reputation for not being married. Mary seemed always alone.

As for being her father's daughter, she represented her family in business affairs and trade with pride. As for not being married, there were many whispers as to why.

The Port of Magdala

Riddled with rickety A-frames hang-drying fish, the place where the salted product was processed and prepared was alive with merchant traffic. Village women cleaned and salted them, boys filled bags, and stacked them. Older men loaded filled bags onto ships, all in a seamless rhythm.

Sarah rushed to the women and children waiting by a tarped table, aligned with others, where merchants sold their wares. Dusting off the table and setting down their bags of goods to trade and sell, Sarah and two field-hands helped Mary with several excited children.

Spotting an older boy among them, a little smaller than the rest, Mary called him out. "You!" she said pointing to the stubby, awkward boy. "Come. What is your name?"

"Josiah," the boy responded bashfully.

"Here," she replied handing him an old sack of salted fish and bread. "Make sure everyone gets some," Mary instructed, rushing them off. The children ran off glad, following the boy.

An assortment of herbs, oils, small and medium clay vessels sat on a table with worn scales and used measuring tools.

"Mary, more trouble!" Sarah called. Mary turned to see her standing with a pregnant woman, her head covered, trying to hide her face. Sitting the woman near the shade by bushels of fish, Sarah turned to Mary, "She asked for your salted balms when I saw her bruises." Pulling the woman's head cover back, cuts and bruises covered her face.

"Again! This must stop, you're with child!" yelled Mary. "Sarah! Bring my balms," she fumed. Sarah hurriedly scanned the table of vessels. The distressed woman winced as Mary covered her wounds with the salt-balm. "I'm so tired," wept the wounded woman. "It's more frequent. We don't know what to do. Our husbands, they tell us we invite it. Our punishment doubles. We fear sending our daughters to chore," she continued, rocking herself in her grief.

"She speaks of road bandits," Sarah explained. "Attacks have increased on the routes, even in the day."

"This savagery, this beating of women!" Mary seethed. "What makes a man strike a woman; a husband **beat** his own wife? Why should we marry? For this?" she lamented, throwing her hands up with frustration.

Suddenly a brawl broke out with thugs crashing on the table near the women. Falling over, screaming, the women landed on top of each other, fish scattering, flopping on them all. Guards rushed arresting the brawlers, beating some down, Barabbas, a murderous rebel leader among them.

"I will kill you! With my bare hands," Barabbas warned resisting the guards who struggled to drag the thief away.

Mary helped the women up, covered in fish. Trying not to laugh at the flopping fish on the wounded woman, Mary saw no one was hurt further by the chaos when Sarah and the woman burst laughing. "Barabbas! One day!" Mary screamed, reaching out to comfort the already injured pregnant woman. "One day, he'll *meet* his match!" she grinned.

The day was a long one. The sun set lazily as Mary retreated near the edge of the pier. She looked, seeing the last of the ship-hands loading their boats. One had caught her attention as he helped an older worker load his loads. Not realizing her gaze, a rowdy group passing by blocked her view.

Agitated, she hollered, "Clear the way!" waving them away.

One male prostitute, a gigolo scarred on the face, turned to see her frustration, "You don't own the port, Mary," he sassed, slyly walking her way. "Join us!" he added with a grinned smile.

"Not today. It's been a long one," Mary responded. "Get out of the *way*, now! Move on!"

"Ship-hands are coming!" he said, turning to see the man she gazed at. "Maybe that one!" He turned back to see her gawking at him and smiled lewdly. "I saw you." Laughing mischievously, he raced back to his group of friends. They walked toward the shore, pointedly looking back to tease her.

Mary returned her wandering thoughts back to the ship-hand she admired but turned to see Sarah's face staring wide-eyed back at her instead. "Mary! I saw you!" whispered Sarah as loud as she could through her clenched teeth. "What are you thinking?"

"I'm ready for a man!" snapped Mary. "A good man, maybe that one!" she said pointing to the ship-hand. "Look how hard he works, Sarah." She smiled, jumping off the stump-stool and heading to the warm waters of the sea. "And he helps the elders!" Mary hollered back.

"Stop!" scolded Sarah.

"They gather tonight on the shore! Guess where we'll be?" Mary's eyes twinkled.

Magdala's Shore

The sun now past, the moon now full, children raced along the waters' edge, splashing up the foam. The bright moonlight beamed across the sea. The sand was still warm in their toes from the day.

Others gathered by a fire, eating and drinking, laughing and sharing memorable moments of their afternoon. Many homeless, prostitutes, and riffraff gathered every night as well as some passing through.

Mary and Sarah among them eating, were known well by all the people. A woman of ill repute and familiar to them drew near with her family and sat with them, jumping into their lively conversation.

"I've heard it said the Healer blesses the wombs of the barren. Still no child, Mary? No child, no husband?" she asked brashly.

"None from my womb, but many through God's kindness," replied Mary.

"How can God favor a sinner?" retorted the woman, laughing.

Mary smiled, thinking of the woman's words for a moment, slightly embarrassed. "One can hope. There is always hope. All I know is though I lack children of my own, I seem to have more-than-enough around me!" she replied softly smirking toward Sarah.

"I am not a child," Sarah smiled sarcastically.

Admittedly, the woman responded, "Yes, children and the young come to you often, I'm aware. It must be a sign of God's favor, even for you."

Mary pressed, curiously inquiring of Him, "What else do they say of the Healer?"

"It is said He is God with us. More than God's own Son, yet He walks among us. A God of the people," the woman paused.

"A God *for* the people," Mary added, intrigued at the growing reports of Jesus.

"Why no man, Mary?" a homeless woman asked, stoking the fire.

"I've had my eye on one," Mary chimed back.

"Your worker is married, from Jerusalem!" the sassy gigolo from the pier hollered out loud. "That ship has gone! Ha! No love again, Mary!" he snorted, laughing.

"Married? Gone?" she huffed, catching Sarah's glaring eyes.

"Jerusalem!" the homeless woman shouted. "The Deliverer goes there often!" she smiled her toothless grin. "He travels to Bethsaida."

"The priests warn he has devils," the gigolo, Avner, shouted. "For He sits with people like us. He sits with sinners like you do, Mary." Moving toward her he leaned in, "They say we serve the god of sin. Jesus says there is only one god. What do you think, Mary?" Mary, repulsed by his fishy odor, moved back and away.

"Come with us, Mary!" the homeless woman begged. "Many of us follow Him despite those who tell us we are not worthy," she urged. "Something happens when He speaks. Miracles!"

"We must be getting back," reminded Sarah, her eyes on Mary as she stood to her feet. "Martha will be cross already when she sees your hair, Mary," Sarah teased.

"Yes!" the homeless woman said aloud. "What happened to it?" she laughed. "I meant to ask."

Embarrassed, Mary ran her hand along her hair, braiding it roughly and replied, "It wasn't supposed to stay on this long. It's henna dye from the port. It may last a while."

Sarah drew close to her smiling, "I warned you not to do it, Mary!"

THE SOUND of NEW LIFE

BETHSAIDA

The routes were alive with excitement as children hurried past the slower adults, trying to help spread the good news. The man who turned water into wine was near and news spread everywhere that it happened near Cana, not far from Nazareth. Further fueling their gladness were the rumors that the one responsible was of the House of David and multiple miracles followed.

The sound of the voice of the Lord thundered across the hillside during a beautiful sermon. "If you feel worn and weary, beaten down, come!" Jesus preached, His voice echoing through the valley. Crowds of people cascading hillslopes, and many children up in trees, pressed to get as close as possible to the Nazarene.

Mary and Sarah emerged from climbing the hill, followed by the group from the shore, many children and riffraff. Josiah ran ahead with a rolled-up fish sack, finding shade. The others followed fast. Mary's countenance became more radiant the nearer she drew to Jesus.

Settling herself to hear His voice, Mary's eyes fixed on Jesus. She's heard much about Him from those touched by Him. Jesus was

17

preaching on the Kingdom of God when she decided to see for herself if what the people said of Him was true. She didn't realize the Holy Spirit had led her to this place at such a critical time in her life. She would never be the same.

Two old women shared the news of Jesus. "Your face is new," one called out to Mary.

"The Man who turned water into wine is here; miracles happen wherever He goes," she beamed.

"He is a magician, that's all!" warned an older, more doubtful, woman. "Miracles? Watch the priests! They claim He's a trickster, a devil!"

"The House of David?" smirked Mary., "Herod fumes at a challenge. His legitimacy before the people remains troubled; they do not accept Rome's right to choose their king." Turning to Sarah she said, "And people follow prophets."

Seventy paired evangelists returned rushing to Jesus excitedly sharing what they had experienced: devils were subject to them, in His Name! Walking at the tail end of the group, Maximin overheard Mary and interrupted, "The people follow because He is Truth." Looking straight at her he asked, "Will you?" Turning to Sidonius, blind from birth, now healed by Jesus, Maximin called out, "We must tell Jesus of John and Herod's brutality." Mary's ears perked up when she overheard the name of Herod. She leaned in to eavesdrop for more.

"This will break His heart," Sidonius added. "He loved His cousin very much." Maximin arrived to where Jesus was with his head bowed, to share the news of John the Baptist's beheading, at Herod's command. Mary observed the Lord grieved as the crowd looked on, growing restless.

"Blessed are they, persecuted for righteousness' sake," Jesus spoke calling out over the crowd. "The Kingdom of Heaven is theirs." Walking among them, touching the frail, He continued, "When you pray, don't be as a hypocrite who prays where *everyone* can see and notice. I tell you, that is their reward. When you pray, don't use empty repetitions as heathens do. They think God will hear them for their many words. Don't be like them!" The disgruntled religious stirred, murmuring among themselves, grabbing Mary's attention. Jesus was unmoved, continuing, "Your Father knows what you need before you ask. So, with all your heart you should pray, asking God like this: 'Our Father in heaven, Holy is Your name. Your Kingdom come! Yours will be done on earth as it is in heaven. Give us this day our daily bread. Forgive us our sins as we forgive those who sin against us. You lead us, not into temptation, but deliver us from evil. Yours is the Kingdom and the power and the glory forever. Amen.' If you forgive others of their sins and wrongdoings, your heavenly Father will forgive you of all yours. But if you cannot forgive others, neither will you be forgiven."

The Sanhedrin turned one by one. Slipping away and having heard enough, they grew hungry, yawning and ready for a nap. Mary saw their increasing unrest and how distracting they were to the people. The crowd stirred when they saw Jesus turn up the mountain to sit with His followers and the women who served Him. All eyes were on Him when He called out to His disciples, "Where are we to buy bread so these may eat? I <u>hear</u> their hunger for more." He smiled.

Peter scoffed, "Two hundred denarii worth of bread would not be enough for each to get a little."

"Nor twice that," replied Stephen, a zealous, fiery follower of Jesus and one of the Seventy. Maximin and Sidonius drew near, alert.

"This boy came prepared," called Andrew pointing to Josiah. Jesus and the disciples turned to see the scruffy boy pulling a piece of dry bread from his fish sack. Mary sat up, observant of their every move, remembering when she had passed it to the boy days ago.

Smiling at the boy, Jesus approached Josiah stooping down face to face and looks inside his bag. Josiah was captivated by the beauty of the Lord and stood speechless before Him. "More than enough," smiled Jesus, touching Josiah's face. Jesus turned to Peter. "Have the people sit," He directed, taking the loaves and fish from Josiah's bag, smiling.

Turning toward heaven, Jesus lifted them for a blessing saying, "Father, thank You for providing bread to eat. And fish, My Father. Thank You!"

Turning to the Twelve He handed the blessing to them who quickly passed it to the people. Swiftly, the loaves and fish began to multiply!

Mary stretched her neck trying to see past the growing rumbles of the crowd. "Do you <u>smell</u> that? It's <u>bread</u>!" she shouted jumping to her feet.

"It's not possible!" The smell of hot, fresh bread blew over the people who erupted in cheers. Loaves of fresh bread appeared everywhere.

"Fish! Mary, there are so many fish!" screamed Sarah, grabbing all she could. The sound of cheers flowed throughout the famished multitude. Many of the feeble and lame jumped to their feet healed, grabbing food. People who were carried to Jesus on bed mats now ran praising God. "This is the Prophet who is to come into the world! He has come! He is here! MESSIAH! JESUS IS LORD!" came the cheers from the grateful multitude as one voice roared, reaching the heavens. Paralytics jumped to their feet with excitement, laughing and crying at the same time, grabbing bread and fish, overwhelmed with joy. They had

not jumped in so long.

Mary, awed with amazement, plopped down with fish multiplying in her lap. "Sarah!" she screamed, laughing. "Help me!" Everywhere you looked fish and bread multiplied to the joy of the erupting crowd. Religious scoffers too grabbed their share, as did the poorest of them all. Everyone, thousands, were fed in moments!

Mary, Sarah, and the old woman sat eating the last of their fish.

"No trick fills my belly like this," chimed the old doubtful woman. "Those priests lied," she smirked, rubbing her belly warmly. All ate to their fill and soon the crowd quieted down.

Mary remained fixed on Jesus, watching Him from a distance. "I am going to meet Him," she blurted, bolting to her feet.

Approaching Jesus and His disciples, He turned looking directly at her and called out, "Gather the remnants. Let nothing be lost." Mary froze in her tracks with a mouthful of bread-fish at His words as if He were speaking directly to her. Tossing the fish bones still in her hands discreetly and swallowing fast, Mary grabbed a nearby basket and filled it with scraps of food. One by one, the disciples gathered edible pieces into baskets.

Mesmerized by His every move, Mary walked toward them, her eyes consuming all that she could of Jesus. As He dismissed the last of the crowd, He blessed the children again and turned up a higher hill, alone.

"Who is this Man?" asked Mary, leaning toward Sarah. "He comforts everyone. Touching the women with care and respect, not afraid to touch the sick and unclean," she said, watching Him disappear behind the grove of trees. "And He heals them all!"

"The old woman said he's called the devil," answered Sarah, watching from behind.

"He's no devil," said Mary. "I've seen this with my own eyes. We must tell Martha." Turning, the two women rushed excitedly toward others already departing for home.

Arriving after nightfall, talk among the villages varied with reports of miracles and unheard-of healings and cures. After visiting with neighbors nearby, Mary and Sarah made their way late into the night. At the sound of dogs barking in the distance, they quietly entered their home. Mary swiftly lit a candle, nudging her sleeping sister.

Carefully gathering her utensils, Sarah prepared washbowls for their feet. Meticulously, she collected salts and oils, bringing them near the foot of the bed-cushions where a frustrated but excited Martha propped herself up. Sarah sat the items on the table. Removing her cloak and garments, Mary uncovered her long flowing hair as Martha turned to see her.

"There is talk of a Deliverer!" Mary finally shared. "A healer and prophet He's called."

Adjusting her eyes to the dim-lit candle Martha turned toward Mary, much to her surprise, "Mary where have you— **what have you** done to your hair? You have no restraint!" yelled Martha, sitting up.

"It's henna sister, it washes!" assured Mary, embarrassed.

"It's red!" shouted Martha under her hot breath. "And I know **you know** it's dark out! It is late and dangerous! **No time** for women to be out," she scolded, eyeing Sarah, as well. "Lazarus will be so cross with you again, sister! Must you rush my aging?" she rattled on.

Mary hushed her sister quickly and moved in to take a seat on the stump-stool at the foot of their cushions and throws. Martha plopped herself up as Mary began to share with her sister all that she had heard and seen for herself.

"You recall the elders have said?" she began in a whisper. "A wedding occurred, where water was turned into wine near Cana. Curious rumors state this same Man claims to be the Son of God! In days He will travel through here. He heals the sick, Martha!"

Her eyes and firm resolve captured Martha's eagerly listening heart. "The priests are furious and adamant that He is a trickster, even a devil, while others of the Sanhedrin stir up great political controversies," she continued. "This Man continues unmoved, sister! He gathers on the hillslopes of the Mountain of Olives and is nearing our coast. Rumors throughout the village, nearer the city's gates and all throughout the port are that Messiah is coming through. He's already left feeding thousands near Bethsaida. The blind can see, Martha! I saw it for myself!" she continued, astonished. Martha sat mesmerized as Sarah took a seat.

"The deaf hear, the lame jump and are walking, sister!" Mary continued.

"Some say He has devils?" asked Martha, wide-eyed.

"Yes, sister but demons come out screaming when He's near! I must **meet** this man," she insisted, a brisk sweeping over her heart.

The swift, sudden movement within her was so strong, she thought almost physical, as she failed to recognize the Lord's first touch on her spirit. Jesus was calling Mary far before they would ever cross paths.

"Well, you better do something about your hair first," smirked Martha smiling and reaching to touch it. "Then it is Him," she added. "He raised the daughter of Jairus not long ago and the suffering woman who bled without ceasing, down the road. Take me to see Jesus, Mary," begged Martha, facing her. "Something tells me we must all come to Him and soon," she insisted, "for now, we must sleep."

Leaning over the small makeshift stack of flat-stones next to the foot of her bed, Martha blew out the small flame. Together the women could be heard whispering their plans in prayerful excitement, which soon turned to prayers of hope sparking their faith.

The quiet of the night, disrupted only by the distant cries of infants and dogs barking at shadows, offered much peace for their sleep that night.

Jesus and Peter Walk on Water

The disciples were fatigued and worn from such an intense day of ministering to the needs of the people. Soon it was dark and Jesus had not yet come to them. With no sign of Him on the way, they gathered at the shore by Peter's boat eager to cross the sea of the beautiful Galilee. They doused the small campfire and loaded the boat of fish and bread remnants gathered in their baskets.

"You should wait! He will be here," complained Maximin.

"It's time to cast off," retorted Peter. "If He wanted to be here, He would!"

Sidonius rushed toward them, calling out, "More come from the region of Tiberius! They seek Jesus for Caesar. He is ill, they say."

"We go now," said Peter turning to Maximin. "I am a fisherman, not a healer." The twelve disciples boarded to cross, launching quickly, not willing to wait for the Lord. Maximin and Sidonius remained with Stephen and others of the Seventy. There was still no sign of Jesus.

Having sailed for several miles, the disciples dozed off quietly. Some slept while John and Andrew talked of the boy with the fish sack. Soon winds stirred up the waters and a heavy, unexpected storm erupted.

"It's a terrible storm ahead!" yelled Peter over the loud gusts of wind. "You were told to wait for Jesus," cried John. "Now, look!"

The sea roughened at the force of the winds, tossing the men and waking the sleeping. They scrambled for oars, rowing hard and struggling desperately when Andrew pointed to an image walking on the surface of the waves, coming near the boat. Screaming and frightened, they perceived the form to be a ghost.

Calmly, yet thunderously, a reassuring voice called out, "It is I. Do not be afraid!" It was Jesus and Peter knew it.

"Lord!" Peter yelled. "If *it is* You tell me to join You **on the water,**" he said leaning the whole of his body over the edge of the boat. The disciples in frozen, shock, stood huddled, staring and speechless.

"Come!" came the commanding invitation from Jesus, His Word covering the surface of the raging waters in a flash.

Peter grabbed the rail of the boat.

Climbing over the edge, steadying himself against the waves, Peter looked at Jesus. Waters rising all around, he set his gaze on His face. His footsteps took their place above the rising current, quickly stopping every wave on the straight path before him. Placing his right foot on the storm-tossed waves, a glass-like sheet emerged, a solid clear path before him marked his steps. The moonlit way illuminated the face of the angry waters.

Amazed at the radiant sheer light brightening Peter's path, the startled disciples clung to each other, gazing at the sight of their eyes. What was happening all around them had never happened before. His confidence rising higher than the waves, Peter stood steady as his brother-disciples tried to balance themselves against the force of the winds and rain. Waters rose, straining to toss the struggling boat. Moving steadily toward Him, Peter pushed off the edge, his hands free before him, reaching for Jesus.

His face set like flint, his gaze set, intent on the eyes of the Master, Peter stepped. Step by step, he inched forward, then more. Step by step, all fear was gone. Now, nearing the Lord, the gap of distance between them closing rapidly, Peter stretched his fingers toward Jesus. He could almost touch His beautiful hands.

Jesus reached for Peter.

A wave fiercely rose pulling Peter's eyes away from the Lord, and he saw the rage and force of the wind and sea surrounding him. Fear pierced his mind and heart and Peter's foot slipped. The sound of the angry sea, the force of the slapping waves against his face and body, Peter sunk fast, crying out with all his might, "Lord, save mmm...!" Plunging deep beneath the waves, Peter could not reach the surface. Wildly suspended, enveloped by the swallowing vacuum of the sea's force, he stretched his faith, failing to reach Jesus' feet, just above his face. His eyes struggled to see and his hands struggled to grasp the Lord when a hand grabbed Peter by his own, yanking him swiftly through the surface of the sea.

Immediately Jesus touched Peter's faith, reaching him before he was swept away. Yanking Peter from the waters that fought to claim the drowning disciple, Jesus brought Peter up and out, to His own dry chest saying, "You of little faith. Why did you doubt?" He smiled holding Peter tight, face to face. With the full weight of his body clutching and clenching Jesus, Peter tried to regain his footing from the movement that wrestled beneath him. Now pale and soaked, the stunned disciple clung to the Lord, a crooked smile lining his face. Taking him by a firm hold, Jesus and Peter walked back together to the boat and climbed in. All the disciples cheered and honored Jesus, saying, "It's true! You *are* the Son of God!"

Gladness erupted among them all as they welcomed the two into the boat, Peter soaked and Jesus not. Taking their garments, they all helped Peter dry, laughing and teasing him for sinking. Immediately, as they rejoiced, the boat they were in was at land to the very place they were headed.

Overcome by the miracle-working power of Jesus, the disciples poured their love and appreciation over Him, some weeping at the mercy of God, amazed at all they had seen. They were growing more as brothers.

Peter sat at the feet of Jesus, stoking the fire, keeping it hot. Overcome by their joy and overwhelmed at the authority of the Lord, the disciples unloaded their provisions briskly. John placed fish on the fire, enough for them all. The disciples prepared to celebrate by breaking bread, as they had grown very hungry and were so very tired.

"Why did you look away, Peter?" Jesus asked, looking straight into the disciple's troubled eyes.

Looking away, Peter took a moment to think of his words honestly, searching his heart. "The sound, the waves," he slowly responded.

"You've done well, Peter. None of that should fill your thoughts or weigh your heart," Jesus encouraged, leaning toward the solemn man.

"No, Lord," Peter replied quickly. "I was afraid. The very thing you teach us not to do, I did. It wars within me, every day."

"I sense it won't be the last time" Jesus smiled; His eyes set on Peter.

Turning to face the Lord, Peter finally asked, "How is it You came to us across the water? How is it the waves carried You?"

"It was you I came across the water for, Peter. It was your faith that called out to Me. That same faith that always calls out to Me. The thing you fear will always come upon you, Peter. You must not fear. It is the weakest part of man's mind and heart. To fear is to not trust God, our Father. Be concerned, but do not give in to fear. God will make perfect what concerns you," Jesus smiled. "Many things trouble you, Peter."

"Yes, Lord," Peter hesitated, turning back to the fire. "Many turn back and no longer walk with You, with us."

Hearing concern in his voice Jesus turned to them all saying with a heavy heart, "Do you want to go away as well?" John, Andrew, and the disciples stopped what they were doing to hear the words of the Lord, sensing the heaviness of those words.

Peter stood to his feet abruptly and loudly asked, "Lord, to whom shall we go? You have the words of life that lasts forever! Your words pierce our hearts and cause us to pause and reflect on our lives, on what is truth! We believe and know that You are the Holy One of God!"

Jesus stood slowly facing Peter, saying, "Did I not choose you, the Twelve? And yet one of you **is** a devil." The disciples stood speechless as if arrested by His words, pondering them wholeheartedly. Looking at each other and knowing within themselves His words rang true, they reclined again, around Him, one by one.

He spoke of Judas, the son of Simon the leper[3], the chief Pharisee. Judas, one of the twelve, would soon betray Jesus.

"Eat and rest well, friends," He encouraged. "Tomorrow we retreat to the outer regions away from the pressing crowds, for a short while." The disciples stood in the quiet, glancing at each other. "Watch and pray," He called back as always, disappearing for the night.

AN UNBELIEVER SHOWS HER FAITH

TYRE/SIDON

Jesus and the Twelve departed from Bethsaida to the region of Tyre and Sidon and a world of pagan, idolatrous people. The Greco-Roman ruled region was wrought with godless paganism and a worldly lust for gain. Within days, word had run through the market that a Healer, a Miracle-Worker, was near. Nearing the place and still along the dry road, Jesus and His disciples heard the cry of a woman, wailing loud and long.

Then, a Canaanite woman emerged hollering for Jesus, saying, "Mercy! Have mercy on me, Son of David! **My daughter is severely demon-possessed! Help me, Rabbi!**" Unmoved, Jesus stayed silent walking past the gate and through the market. Relentlessly begging to no avail, the sweaty, disheveled woman, her face pierced with symbols of her gods, went after James then Andrew.

The disciples who tired of her urged John to tell Jesus, saying, "Send her away Lord, she comes after us now!"

---

[3] Globalchristiancenter.com/Christian-living/lesser-known-bible-people/31288-simons-son-judas

Jesus unmoved answered John, saying, "I was sent to **the lost sheep** of Israel; not this. "

The woman fell to His feet wrapping her face in His hem, saying, "Lord, help me! I have no one!" Looking up, hoping to see His face, instead He ignored her when she cried, "She hates me, Jesus! My daughter hates me!" wailing with all her heart.

None of this moved the Lord. Instead Jesus answered, "It is not good to take the children's bread and throw it to dogs."

The Canaanite woman, distraught on her face before Him, calmed herself down and replied weeping, "Yes, Lord, this is true. But even the *little dogs* get to eat all the crumbs that fall from their masters' table." Looking back to Him, she whispered, "All I need are a few crumbs, Lord, not many."

Slowly, Jesus turned to look at her dry, cracked face and smiled on her saying, "Woman, your faith has freed your daughter! Let it be to you as your heart has desired."

Jumping to her feet, the woman erupted in her native tongue, rejoicing while the stunned disciples stood back, staring. "Thank you, Jesus!" she wept, grabbing and kissing His hands, repeatedly. "I will bring her to You soon!" she called, disappearing into the mixed crowd of idol worshipers.

Jesus turned to the still-stunned disciples, saying, "I hear hunger. We return to Capernaum." The woman's daughter was healed that very hour.

CAPERNAUM

Jesus, preaching on the hillside early in the morning, could be heard as the sound of His voice thundered through the valley. "If you are worn out, beaten down by this world, come!" He called over the growing crowd of large groups that came. From as far as the eye could see, travelers brought broken, distressed, sick, and dying loved ones in hope of receiving His touch. Desperate people brought desperate people; the blind tried to help the blind. Everyone followed the voice of the Lord. "Come to Me!" His voice echoed, "Come, all who are weary and worn! Learn from Me! I will give you rest for your tired souls! Come!" Jesus called repeatedly, waning not.

People from every corner of the region brought their sick on mats and carts. Children, the frail elderly, and paralytics had found a glimmer of hope in the form of this seemingly ordinary Man. Unlike other men, this one had power from heaven emanating through His every word.

Following near the outer edges of the crowds that gathered, Mary pressed to hear the words of Jesus, making her way through the crowd. "He's talking to me, it seems," she shouted excitedly to Martha following close behind.

"You look ridiculous!" Martha called, referring to Mary's red hair. "He's talking to *all* of us," she smiled at Mary, mesmerized by the sound of Him whose voice ran through her.

Oblivious to her own sister, servant, or others who had also gathered, Mary moved through the multitude of people. Finding a place to sit just behind the Lord, she was soon captivated by His presence. Her heart, her mind were awake to His words with understanding. His word softened her heart. She never realized how much it had hardened. Not having her mother when she needed her most had left deep wounds within her. She never fully heard the harshness in her tone when she spoke, or how constant and defensive her mannerisms had become. Her words could cut *deeply* when impassioned or enraged at injustice. Self-control was *far* from the unbridled tongue of Mary, the Magdalene. The sound of His voice softened her edges, at the entrance of His word.

"Love your enemies," Jesus' voice echoed through the valley reaching every ear. "And pray for those who persecute you."

"That is unheard of!" blurted Martha. "Who can love like that? Pray for your persecutors?" Pausing to reflect on those words and glancing toward the disciples, Mary saw an imperial carriage coming up the hill. Claudia, the wife of Pilate, Roman Prefect of Judea under Tiberius, rode regally. Though veiled and shrouded, she was graceful and beautifully simple, as well as being the daughter of the Emperor's wife, *Julia.*

"Pilate's wife, do you see her?" nudged Mary, pointing discreetly. Sarah tried to see where Mary gestured, saying, "No. Where?"

Mary leaned out of her way. "In the carriage," pointed Mary, noticing Joanna. Joanna was walking to greet Mary, the Mother of Jesus, and the company of women who served Him. Also, noticing Mary across the way, Joanna gestured her "hello" to Mary. The courts, from Pilate to Herod and even Caiaphas, knew Mary well, and knew of her family's wealth in the region.

"Mother, the wife of Pilate is here, Claudia," Joanna whispered in Mother's ear, pointing her way.

"Something troubles her Joanna," she replied seeing the elite carriage. "Why would she come? See to her please."

"And the Magdalene," Joanna added, gesturing Mary's way. "More continue to come."

Turning to see Mary, Mother smiled, "They need to come; *all* do."

"I shall return," Joanna responded, dismissing herself and making her way through the growing crowd followed by Susanna.

"Claudia, how do you fare?" called Joanna.

The regal, shrouded woman revealed a beautiful scarf made of ivory silk, lovingly lined with gold and silver; it was very special to her.

"For the Mother of Jesus," Claudia replied, "please, and prayers. My uncle, the Emperor, is ill."

Taking the scarf Joanna assured her, "I will share your request and deliver your gift, how beautiful."

Leaning in privately, Susanna greeted the Emperor's niece, saying, "It is good that you are here, Claudia."

"That we are all here," smiled Claudia. "His words have a way of piercing one's heart. They cut deeply, it seems," she added.

Smiling, Joanna agreed, "Yes, and shedding light and truth for us all. I'll see to it Mother receives your gift and your request for prayers."

Returning to the company of women, Joanna and Susanna presented Mother with Claudia's scarf. Placing it around her neck, Joanna whispered, "A gift from Claudia, Mother. She asks for prayers for Tiberius."

"An offering!" replied Mother gladly. Receiving the gifted scarf, she admired it, saying, "Much more than a gift! We can offer prayers for Caesar, yes! God can heal and deliver even a hater of His people!" Turning toward Claudia, Mother gestured her gratitude with a gentle smile. Mary curiously observed every move the women made, turning her attention back to Jesus. She smiled at his gentle countenance and patience.

Blessing the crowd, Jesus noticed children being shunned by a group of religious leaders and walked toward them. "With God there are no differences," Jesus called out, encouraging. "Only with man. So, love your enemies," He continued.

"No differences?" whispered Mary.

Hearing her, Jesus turned saying, "God is love. God is kindness. Is it so difficult to show kindness to everyone? Do not all people deserve acts of kindness? There is no honor in showing love or kindness only to those like you," Jesus pressed, seeing Mary.

Now, turning back His attention to the many children who were being mistreated, Jesus smiled, "Pray from your heart to God and He will hear you. Don't be a hypocrite with loud, repetitious, long-faced prayers," He continued looking directly at each face and stretching His face in gesture. The children burst into laughter, then Mary, so much that her laugh embarrassed Sarah. Trying to contain her laughter, Mary moved next to her sister and the women gathered. Jesus, overjoyed, turned up the hill as the end of another day drew near. Turning once more to bless them as He departed, He looked over the multitude and saw Mary, again.

With disdain Simon glared at her, still chuckling about Jesus's gestures. "Stubborn sinners," he smirked, turning away.

"Mary!" scolded Martha, standing and facing Simon.

"I did nothing to provoke him, sister," Mary said defensively. "Jesus said there is no difference between us, with God. Why is it that some people consider themselves more highly than they ought to?" she lamented to Martha, sliding her look toward Simon.

Seeing Jesus turn up the higher hill, she looked at Sarah and Martha. "We must follow Jesus," she stressed, gathering her things to leave.

The sun now set, the crowd dispersed, Jesus stood facing the sea alone. The disciples boarded Peter's boat as Andrew approached the Lord, "This was a huge feeding, Rabbi. The people hungered much here as well." Peter drew near, asking, "Where to now, Teacher?"

Looking to the horizon, Jesus panned the sea, calmly closing His eyes. "Magdala," he smiled.

The teachings of Jesus were like nothing ever heard before. No one had ever spoken with assurance, knowledge, or passion for what was right and true, or boldness to unveil the wrong and the evil. No one had ever addressed the crowds with patience, love, or compassion. It was compassion that moved Jesus to miracles. It was mercy that called Him to Magdala.

THE LAKE ATTACK

A few days later, coming from the direction of the Great Lake, not too far from the sea, a field-hand ran desperately to gather help for one who had been assaulted. Mary, the strongest of the women in their village and like a sister to them all, was the one they turned to the most. Fearing the worst, Mary followed fast, joined by several others. Upon seeing the wounded woman on the ground bleeding, Mary was taken aback by the ferocity of the attack. Seeing the familiar woman had been left for dead, she uttered a roar of anguish from deep within and ran to the bleeding, motionless body. Her fears recalled the many threats women in the region faced daily and multiple warnings from Martha trying to keep them safe. It was always dangerous for women to be alone.

"They pursue and take our women at will!" Mary screamed. "Daughters of the meekest among us as well! It matters not! No one hears them! **They know** to keep silent. These savages take our lives away to breathe! To hope. To live. To love! To gather simple provisions, we must plan and plot our way far too often!" Frustrated and enraged Mary could hardly contain herself. Enraged at the helplessness of their cry for these things to stop and to change, Mary was angered to tears and overwhelmed.

Kneeling near the wounded woman, Mary cried out, "Who can endure suffering this cruelty?" Her crackled voice screamed from deep within her soul. Touching her friend's bleeding and battered face, Mary tried to comfort the bleeding woman.

The field-hands stepped forward. "We must take her home, ma'am," one said, the other lifting her ravaged body and carrying her to Mary's house.

With servants tending the wounds of the beaten woman now asleep from her weeping, Mary took salts from her pouch, adding some to the warm water. Slowly swirling, she added medicinal oils and myrrh.

"I recall my years as a young girl watching skilled artisans and alchemists," she shared softly with Martha.

"You were an avid, astute listener," Martha responded. "Absorbing with your eyes and heart, much like you do now listening to Jesus." Servants helped with cleaning and binding the wounds of the woman as Martha stood watch, praying.

"Why is it the harder we try to do good, to get close to God, something always pulls back like an unseen evil?" Mary asked with a heavy heart, her eyes on the wounded woman.

Taking a deep breath, Martha softly responded, "Evil needs no reason to strike, Mary. It eats away like a plague. It is the way of the world."

"It is not our way, this must **stop!**" Mary snapped back in a loud whisper. "If so, we would not tire of it and need things to change! This treatment of women, this hate!" Where does it come from?"

"You must learn to do as you are expected," Martha stressed. "It is the way of our world. It has always been this way. Women do as they are told, nothing more, seen, not heard. You are a dreamer, Mary," Martha added. "You look for a man not from this world, all men lord over their women. We are to be in submission and without a thought to ourselves. You are here to serve your man: husband, father, bro——"

"Have you lost your mind? Where does that law come from that they may lord over us at will, and harmful?" Mary snapped, flustered in her frustration. "Men do not differ from women so much as they want us to believe! All throughout our day, we fuss, toil and labor, male and female with no difference! When the day is over, it exhausts us, male and female with no difference. Except for our blessing to bear children from our own womb, although I have none, they are no different. That is one difference they can never have."

"Mary!" choked Martha, her hand to her mouth. "My mind and heart cannot imagine <u>anything</u> like a man wombed with child!" Holding their mischievous smiles, the two sisters looked over their shoulders, back on the wounded woman and friend, resting in quiet.

"You are more than a sister, you are my closest friend, Martha," smiled Mary, grateful for their growing closeness.

"And you, mine," Martha replied drawing her sister close.

"I cannot bear this evil," Mary whined.

Looking solemnly at Mary, Martha continued, "Please know Mary, the world has a mind of its own, a spirit of its own. There are many who belong to it and its ways. Your strength comes from knowing you are not of this world **if** you belong to God. That truth will forever be a force of friction within you. Your best is to love and serve from the heart those less strong. Leave all change to God. He is fair." Martha smiled, trying to calm her defensive sister.

"I cannot belong to God any more than I already do," Mary pushed back. "I am *outcast.* As a child I knew *closeness* to God, but that was long ago."

"That is where you make your *greatest* mistake, Mary," interrupted Martha, correcting her sister. "If God is your father why would He cast you out?"

Responding quickly, Mary insisted, "Not all fathers are good! Not all men are good! I don't *fare well* with men and I'm sure God is one! Men think of me too strong for a woman, and perhaps I am. Loss has a way of hardening a woman, I guess."

"It's your mouth!" scolded Martha in a nearly raised voice. "Your attitude! You can be unruly, Mary. Outspoken, yes! Outcast, no. That mouth of yours, woman!" she fumed. "You need to set a guard over it!"

"A woman who speaks what her thoughts reveal is unruly? Strange," argued Mary. "Even when we are correct, we are told we are not. We're worth *less* than goats, sister, *admit* it!"

"You are truly a woman with issues, girl," Martha replied holding her chuckle. "I am aware of the rumors of some. You've embraced life away from God. There is where your sin lies. Not too much for God, though," Martha encouraged. "Let's send everyone home, now. We leave for Jerusalem in days, then Bethany. Lazarus waits."

"I won't be returning to Magdala, Martha, not to stay," Mary finally settled. "There is much trouble for me here, for us," she continued pointing to the wounded servant. "My heart is in Bethany. After our work in Jerusalem, I intend to stay there and settle with Lazarus for a while."

"Then Bethany it is!" beamed Martha gladly. "I'll join you for the stay and make preparations. We'll send word to Lazarus right away."

Their world had grown strangely smaller it seemed, the closer they got to the Lord. With scornful mockers gathering in cliques all around her, Mary would hear them whisper as she passed them on the way. Her appreciation of the Lord would not allow her to be kept in shame or hindered any longer. She learned to encourage herself through many moments of harsh and unfair, unkind treatment. She found strength and convicting reassurance of God's love for her and her people, through the words of Jesus.

A woman before her time. Not quite *fitting in* with the rule of law or the abuse of man, much *like* the Lord.

CAUGHT IN THE ACT

JERUSALEM

Overrun with a mix of traffickers, Jerusalem's port was filled with religious elite shadowing the needy. Mercy was far from this place. The horrors of slaves traded or sold flourished as *normal*, daily occurrences. Traders on routes brought rarities from throughout the region; the King's Highway was near. Everything was for *sale* on the ports.

When they arrived, Sarah directed the field-hands to unload the cart. "These vessels are for trade," she hollered, pointing to the clay pots. "Take these to the perfumers. Go in my place," she instructed the workers and ran to catch up to Mary.

Mary walked ahead through the crowd avoiding snickers, lowering her head, tightening her wrap. Roman guards recognized her and moved in her direction. One guard stepped out to block the women calling out, *"Have you no husband?"* The women halted, startled. "It's been long since I've seen you in Jerusalem," he continued nearing Mary. He loomed over her smaller stature intimidating her to face down and away. "I never see you with a man. *Lazarus* away?" he snarled. Another brash, rude guard approached Sarah with lust in his eyes. The women dared not turn to see their faces.

Suddenly and without warning, a disruption broke out among the merchants distracting the guards, giving the women a chance to escape. Weary of the constancy of her nagging, Mary ignored the hurtful comments and rushed on her way. Sarah sensed her frustration and turned to the thoughtless men, who returned their lustful look to Mary. "Keep ignoring me, *Magdalene!* I'll see you again!" threatened the foul guard.

Mary's brisk walk toward the tax booth paused when she recognized the ship-hand she admired. Unloading goods from a ship, he was vigorously moving the heavy, stacked cargo. Mary tried to hide her stare spotted by dallying merchants who vied for her affection.

They called to her, drawing attention, embarrassing her. "No, love for me today, Mary?" one trader tested.

"I don't know which Mary you are calling! There is no love for you today, sir, or tomorrow. Not from this Mary!" she replied waving him off, unamused. The merchant waved, smiling with hidden deceit. His sheepish grin concealed his truth when Mary perceived it and yelled back, "Go to work!"

His halfhearted hand raised, waved as he mocked, whispering to himself, "One day. Not today." Mary was not aware of the two bandits who followed her closely. They saw her wealth and despising her mouthy arrogance, decided to wait for her one mistake.

"Poor man," responded Sarah. "Must he try so hard?" she chuckled, but Mary ignored her. "Married, I'm sure," added Sarah, referring to the dallying old merchant. "Poor wife!" she laughed loudly. Mary looked back to the ship-hand she admired, though, not giving ear to Sarah. They made eye contact, smiling with caution, not wanting to draw attention from others.

Aware of her interest in the man, not her husband, Sarah pulled Mary back to reality. The watchful bandits noticed. "Mary!" Sarah snapped, pulling Mary's arm.

"I hoped he would turn my way," Mary confided with no shame. "And he has!" Having none of it, Sarah pulled her along firmly. "He is married!" hushed Sarah. "Remember?" Approaching the tax booth, Mary stopped at seeing a homeless woman nearly hidden and gave her a bit of bread, fruit, and a small rolled-up mat. The woman gratefully touched Mary's face, kissing her hand.

"It's good to see you again, my friend," Mary greeted the old homeless woman. "This is from Martha, for comfort," she smiled, tucking a handmade doll at her breast. The grateful old woman's softened countenance beamed as she took the woven doll with a henna painted smile and bright eyes.

Turning to Mary tearfully, she whispered, "Thank you," kissing her hand, again.

"I will see you again, soon," smiled Mary.

"Which properties?" the taxman called. Arriving at the booth Mary pulled out worn papyrus scrolls and a small old, leathery pouch.

"Magdala, Jerusalem and Bethany," replied Mary, passing him the old wrinkled scrolls and the weathered leather pouch of coins. Stepping back, she looked around and saw the bandits standing with thugs and riffraff laughing and loitering near the pier. One bandit, an older man, smiled at Mary.

Ignoring him, she asked the taxman, "Where is the taxman Levi?" The older taxman answered, "Gone, said he'll not return. Followed the leader, Jesus." He then returned the scrolls now marked, and the empty pouch.

"Jesus?" Mary asked softly.

"Yes, he left everything and went," the taxman replied rudely. Mary left the booth tucking her scrolls and pouch away and neared a table of herbs and dried flowers, picking up a very large bundle of myrrh. Paying the merchant, she heard Sarah calling. "Quickly, Mary! The workers come!" Turning away, Mary quickened her pace, making her way through the crowd toward the waiting carts. The bandits followed in a distance, watching her every move.

Loading goods and filled clay pots, a field-hand carrying a small covered item approached Mary. "A gift from the perfumer, 'for lady Mariam of Magdala,' he said," reported the field-hand. Helping her board the cart, he handed her the gift.

Mary removed the woven burlap-type wrap to discover an old wooden box and opened it. Wrapped tightly with linen and tied with a cord, Mary took what felt like a long, heavy object and loosened the thick, red thread. A beautiful long green alabaster flask lined, semi-translucent and radiant, felt cold in her hands. She opened the bottle made of soft stone, inhaling the aroma of fresh spikenard. "How beautiful," she smiled as Sarah boarded the cart. Mary showed the beautiful flask to her, admiring its translucence, pouring some amber-colored oil onto her palm. Feeling its thickness and smelling it again, Mary smiled, whispering, "I know what to use this for!" Closing her eyes, she inhaled the *gently strong*, aromatic fragrance.

The field-hands rushed to board, after loading the filled clay pots. "Let's go!" yelled Sarah, and they eagerly made their way home tired and hungry from the day.

Arriving at Martha's, Mary entered followed by Sarah, who helped remove her head cover. Resting against the door, Mary was glad to be home when suddenly a frantic Martha stormed in, "What have you done?" she yelled. "They will drag you from Jerusalem and stone you dead! Men calling your name out loud, and who is this *ship-hand* I hear you look for?" Startling the women, Martha was furious, disheveled, and distraught. Mary stood back speechless and Sarah slipped away.

"I've done *nothing*, sister!" Mary cried.

"People talk more than you think," hollered Martha. "It's reached Jerusalem! They say you are without restraint! Rude!"

Shocked, Mary replied, "It's not true! No one will believe it! There are *many Mary's* here! You worry so much, sister!" she continued nervously, setting down the boxed flask.

Sarah returned to serve her water quickly, leaving the room discreetly. "I worry for you!" yelled Martha. "You're out late. You sit with sinners and women who... I can't even say it!" she fumed, slapping her hand over her mouth.

Mary tried to explain, "I know the people, Martha! I trade on the ports and help the wounded. I try to remember the children."

Refusing to hear excuses, Martha blurted, "Whatever it is, it *follows* you! Examine yourself! Ask yourself what it *might* be. You're unruly and defensive, show respect!" persuaded Martha, angrily.

Mary turned to her sister in surprise, "What does that mean? I respect! I deal with unruly people, sister," Mary stressed, trying to explain.

Peeking from around the corner of the door Sarah whispered, "It's true, I'm a witness! The people can be harsh." She then retreated behind the doorway, again, quietly.

Gathering herself, Martha looked sternly at Mary, "Jerusalem's laws are enforced more *rigidly* than in Magdala, Mary. You must be respectful of the ways. Limit your time there," she warned, pleading.

"We must return, Martha," Mary explained. "We came for more supplies. Workers go before us to Bethany now. They wait for us."

"I will go with you," Martha replied. "Jesus is in the city and I want to hear and see Him more."

Seeing Martha's countenance soften, Mary calmed herself, "The carts will be *too full,* sister. We'll return for you afterwards, *then* I'll take you to find Jesus," she promised.

Mary, Sarah, and the field-hands departed for Jerusalem. Mary, quiet and heavyhearted, kept to herself braiding her hair and Sarah gazed steady on the road ahead, searching her heart for the right words. Seeing Martha wave from her doorway, Mary returned a hesitant wave, saying, *"I know what she says is true."*

Sarah, taking Mary by the hand and squeezing lovingly, whispered, "I know you do." Taking a turn on the bend in the road, the field-hands drove the women and cargo straight to Jerusalem.

Surrounded by obvious abusers of her uneventful world, Mary continued to avoid those who harassed her and other women. From her former sinful indulgences and weaknesses, rumors had swirled for so long about those who continued to fail at winning her attention. Traders on routes, wealthy and provisional, often attempted to woo the beautiful Mary. Vulgar men, married or not, lusted in vain over her, often with her unaware.

Mary was a simple woman; simply complicated. In a time when women were not among the taught or skilled, Mary *was*. In a time when dreams and hopes were strangers, Mary held hers *close* to her heart. In a time when the worth and value of a woman was less than cattle, Mary knew how *wrong* it was. It was a time not prepared for someone like Mary, the Magdalene. She warred within herself, as all women did, to allow the abusive rule of law and man to be as it was. She could hardly contain herself. Mary was different. The weight of the cares of her day would not allow her to keep silent, as all she could do was long, with desperate desire, for change. Hers was a desperate desire for love.

Loneliness lay in wait for a chance to capture empty hearts. Mary's every attempt to resist for the sake of true love would often fail and her rumored reputation grew steadily more sinful. Mary was trapped.

Well past the age of marriage, she continued to suffer reproach, humiliation, and shameful ostracizing. It wasn't enough that she missed her mother, Mary could not recall being told she was loved. Of course, she was loved *dearly,* but could not recall being told so personally. She

43

never had a boyfriend, as a young girl; her culture would not allow it. Her *father* would not allow it! And *then* there was Lazarus!

But, on the day they caught her, love was far from her mind and heart. They had always known where she would be, and when. What else did anyone think she would be busy doing when they caught her in the *very act* of adultery? The merchant ports were almost a second home to her, but it was also the place she found *most* of her trouble.

Reaching the end of herself that day, loneliness crept her way. A culture where a woman was judged and found guilty of adultery for looking at a man flirtatiously, or for being *perceived* by another as doing so. For being uncovered, unaccompanied by your husband, father, brother, or male relative, they would *stone* you to death. For using *foul language* or looking at a man *not your husband*, the same fate. They dragged out women, past the walls of the city, and *one by one,* the villagers cast huge stones *at and on* them, to their death. Not just women, but men as well, if caught. A woman, though, only needed an *accuser* or two.

Arriving in Jerusalem, the women rushed toward the market, the field-hands way ahead of them. Without warning, a man abruptly stepped in front of Mary blocking her rudely. "Where are you going, Mary?" snarled the bandit from the market. "You don't look my way like you do others; why is that?" he glared, closing the space between them lewdly and brash.

Suddenly, a familiar man, the second bandit from the market, ran past her yelling back, "A woman worth stoning." He pushed Sarah down and grabbed her bag. Another thug emerged from the shadows and hollered, "A lesson for all the others!" Violently, the hands of many men grabbed Mary, ripping her garment, nearly revealing her nakedness. A barrage of men, some familiar, yelled for the stoning of Mary. Tripping over their feet, Mary fell, hitting her head on the cold, stone market floor.

She thought she knew them, sons and brothers, fathers, uncles. She knew their wives and daughters, having mended many wounds. Many knew Mary as well and had *reason* to want her silenced. "She was a mouthy, un-submissive sinner," some said. Others feared she knew what they had done against their own people: women within the city's gates, some their own servants, some of them *children.*

She had been near Jesus lately though, and often. Close enough to hear His words and feel His power. Following through crowds everywhere He went, *as often as she could,* she learned quickly what evil and sin were. Mary was awake to how deceived she and the people had been for as long as she could remember. She desired more for herself and knew in her heart, if she stayed close to the Lord, she would succeed. "I can rescue many," she thought and soon believed. Doubt held Mary close enough to keep her bound, though, as she vigilantly guarded herself hope deferred. "He's like the others; I just don't know how," she would say, talking herself out of pursuing Him fully. Sarah wobbled to her feet in a daze.

"To the feet of Jesus!" they yelled with raised voices and fists to the heavens that dry, dusty day. Yanking her up off her feet and over their own shoulders, Mary fought back to help herself. Sarah tried to reach her.

It was the time of the temple gathering and everyone knew Jesus would be there, so instead of dragging her to the prison, they dragged her to the Lord. The angered priests and Pharisees pointing the way, sought to find cause against His judgment of her. They would use Mary against Him.

Time slowed to a slow crawl as face after face came before her, lifting her again and again. The sun beating down on her, they hurled her over grabbing hands and fists of so many men that day, pulling and shoving her from parts of her body that had never been touched that way before. "Adulteress! Stone the sinner!" the mob demanded. "Stone her!

She is unclean!" they drooled, ready to see her dead. Sarah pushed through the crowd with all her might and rushed for the temple and Jesus.

Their fierce anger for her blazed past the scorching heat of that searing day overpowering her as she fell to their feet again, their sandals pinching her hands and fingers, trampling her long, black hair. Grabbing for their garments she struggled to stand ripping a red cloak off one man when gnarly hands reached through the crowd taking her by the hair, "This way," they pulled. "Bring her this way through the courts," they yelled, ripping at her as her earring fell to the dust. Mary was dying.

She knew Jesus was in the city.
She knew she would see Him face to face.
She did not know He would love her, like no other.

A growing crowd of hopeful seekers gathered early in the morning in Jerusalem. The temple was the place where Jesus's voice could be heard. "Drink of Me the fountain of living water and never thirst again," He preached with passion. Several disciples, Peter and John, Salome and Joanna also accompanied Him, listening intently along with those desiring to know more about truth and holiness.

Peering through cracks and crevices just to get a glimpse of her ragged, storm-tossed body being dragged to the temple, no one dared help her.

The loud, angry crowd got the attention of those gathered to listen to Jesus, as temple guards rushed toward the noise. Sarah burst in, breathless and desperate, slamming the gates to the temple wide open just as they dragged Mary in, forcing her through, by her matted hair.

Pressing to hear their scoffing shuffles, as if for a moment she forgot what was happening, she wiped the snot and tears from her smeared face gently as if no one could see her. Pulling broken twigs and leaves from her long, tangled hair, she tried to sit, tried to *still* her trembling composure.

The whispers shushed through the shocked crowd came to a dead silence. A gentle breeze and unexpected wind, the dust briskly cleared when the crowd suddenly seized itself. Jesus was standing.

Facing the ground, Mary removed the spec from her eye when suddenly she set her gaze on the feet of the Lord. She touched her bruised cheek. Stunned beyond belief, she lowered her eyes to the dust. Frozen in time, beads of sweat dripped over her blood-scratched face. Tangled and tossed, Mary sat in the dirt, alone. No one could help her.

The beautiful Mary Magdalene, a daughter of Abraham, lay in the dust, a single tear falling down her dirt-smeared face. Bony fingers reached to stand her, jerking her up to her scratched feet. For the first time Mary saw Jesus face to face: His, as if suspended in love, hers, bruised and bleeding.

"Teacher!" scoffed the loud Pharisee, his voice echoed through the court. "This woman," looking at Mary, "this *adulterous* woman has been **caught** in the very act! You <u>know</u> in the law of Moses we are *commanded* to **stone women like this!**" He turned his look to Sarah still holding the gate, shocked and afraid. "What do You say, Rabbi?" he bellied sarcastically, turning to Jesus. Staunchly flanked by the Sanhedrin stealthily in the background, Simon's bolt of arrogance impressed him alone. He quickly looked away from Jesus, shame descending on his stony face. They wanted to test the Lord and have Him charged for a wrong judgment.

Afraid to breathe, Mary could hear the silence falling over the entire courtyard. Jesus bent down, writing in the dust; Mary could see His finger. Midway through completing the message, Jesus, His voice thundering through the chambers, abruptly stood saying, "You without sin," looking at Simon, then her accusers, "Cast the first stone!"

And once more He bent down and wrote on the ground, picking up where He left off, His finger carefully and deliberately spelling out what He knew to be true. Thoughts and images raced through Mary's mind at the words of the Lord. She rushed through the files of her memory, unable to imagine anyone in the place who qualified when the movement from the crowd took her thoughts toward her unimaginable victory. "Is it possible?" she wondered. All time ceased in its place as she struggled to inhale for fear of waking from this dream. *Was she about to be forgiven?*

Lingering at the border of His presence, gathered with so many *desperate, hurting people,* just to *hear* His message of love and forgiveness, left her longing for her own. Moments forever frozen in time when she felt her heart pull her to trust Him more, long before this horrible day. *Why did she delay?* How many times she moved toward Jesus only to be hindered by relentless stalkers vainly working to pull her aside for themselves, despite her desire and efforts for change.

Hearing the piercing truth of Jesus's words, the restless crowd moved, beginning with the older ones. Thumps repeatedly hit the dusty floor, stone upon stone crash-landing around her feet. Jesus wrote in the dust unmoved.

One *sole* pair of feet, fringed at the hem, moved slowly toward Mary, dropping a large stone. Simon walked away. Mary knew they meant the stones for her, each one of them.

Jesus stood, alone with her before Him, "Woman," He whispered, approaching the weeping, wounded Mary. "Where are your accusers? Has no one condemned you?" He tenderly inquired. Captured by the majesty of peaceful calm that descended over her mind and heart, she lifted her face to His.

"No one Lord," Mary whispered in stunned disbelief.

Jesus, full of compassion, looked deep into her exhausted, tear-filled eyes saying, "Neither do I condemn you. Go, sin no more."

He moved toward her, whose face was buried in her hands, weeping and ashamed, and took her into His arms. She could not recall being held so lovingly and defended. Mary was overcome with the events of the hour and the presence of the Lord. All she could do was sob at His chest.

Taking His garment, the Lord covered her, wrapping her securely. As the beauty of His linen garment wrapped itself around her, the old red shawl, *snatched from her attacker,* fell dead to the dust. Sarah rushed to Mary comforting her, and Joanna, quietly surrounding them, slowly made their way through the courtyard.

Salome drew near to Jesus, *"What would You have us do, Rabbi?"* she asked, quietly. The other disciples who had come with Jesus looked on with surprise still on their faces.

"Bind her wounds. I will see her shortly," He replied instructing His daughter-disciple.

"Yes, Lord," Salome whispered, turning to catch up quickly and quietly with the women and Mary, Sarah leading them out. Only the slight echo of their whispered prayers and shuffling of feet sounded through the courts.

The weapons of hate and shameful injustice were that of a murdering spirit, forming against her that day without success, for reason of the Lord. For the first time, Mary had experienced a *promise kept* from a Man Who would soon die for her sins. For the first time, a woman had been defended against the rule of religious law and man. Before a drop of His blood had been shed, Mary was forgiven! But was she *free?*

Jesus turned to the crowd and gawking disciples, reminding them of the words of Isaiah, saying, "'A bruised reed, He'll not break, a smoldering wick, He'll not quench'... mercy *and* justice are needed. I came to heal the sick and set captives free!" All who were there agreed.

SEVEN DEMONS – Delivered

Safe at Martha's home, Mary, her face and arms cut and bruised blended salts and oils for her wounds. Sarah, Martha, and Salome helped, as her troubled mind raced questioning.

"Why if I am a sinner would He spare stoning me?" she asked.

"You've been forgiven, Mary," replied Salome.

A knock at the door sent Sarah to answer when Mary oddly responded, "He is the most beautiful Man I've ever seen, though. Is He married?"

Stunned at the words and sound coming from her Martha replied at once, "Mary! What are you saying?"

When Sarah opened the door, Peter and John entered, then Jesus. Seeing Him, Mary bolted excitedly rushing for Him but halted, falling to her knees face down just before she reached Him. Martha, Sarah, and Salome stood back shocked.

"Every man needs a woman," slithered the tongue of the devil speaking through Mary, her voice now shallow.

Jesus, unmoved, approached her putting His hand on the back of her head firmly. Salome prayed.

"Devil of lies," came the voice of the Lord.

Mary fell back hard, slithering on the floor, her eyes glazed over glaring straight at Jesus. "I know what you want Jesus," slithered the liar. "Lust of the eyes and flesh, pride of life, I have caught you," Jesus addressed the adversary. Mary's foamed mouth smiled back. Martha and Sarah stood stunned. Peter and John prayed and Jesus approached Mary, "Foul, unclean spirits, love of the world, let her go!" He commanded.

Flipping over and slamming, face-down, Mary vomited violently as a dark, foul presence left her, leaving her body limp. Slowly,

Mary moved moaning, wiping her face. "Forgive me, Rabbi, forgive me," she cried, ashamed and exhausted.

Kneeling at her side Jesus brushed back her hair and wiped her tears taking her face in His hands. "Now Mary, you are free," He smiled, standing her up.

This prodigal daughter could never return to the home of her father, for he had passed long ago. Nor, would she know marriage, like other girls. Most girls twelve to sixteen were already married or having children, *not Mary.* Delivered of this disgrace, hers would become a lifelong dedication, *as if married* to the Lord in gratitude, through her love. Mary would never return to Magdala again. She would follow Jesus for the rest of her life. Those who are forgiven of much, *love much.*

BETHANY—Lazarus

Field-hands drove a cartful of goods heading to Bethany. Martha and Sarah rode gladly, with Mary bandaged and sore. Approaching the house, excited children rushed waving, eagerly greeting them. Lazarus emerged gladly from the age-old home, calling out, *"Welcome, come on! Come!"* as Mary tried to conceal her face. The field-hands parked the cart right in front of Lazarus. Mary had no place to hide and a lot of explaining to do.

Noticing her bandages, Lazarus looked to Martha, concerned. "What happened to you?" he asked sarcastically, his eye of concern now on Mary.

Sarah served more food, setting the water down and took a seat next to Mary, still nursing her wounds. Lazarus, concerned for her, continued to inquire of her attack in Jerusalem and deliverance through Jesus.

"This girl was foaming at the mouth! *In my house!"* exclaimed Martha.

"Must you say it like that, Martha?" complained Mary.

"It's the truth; and your eyes! Like a rabid dog! Jesus freed her!" Sarah chimed.

Lazarus leaned back. "I've heard of this before, but not to anyone close to me. How do you feel?" he asked his solemn sister.
"Beat. Like I have awakened from a dream," she answered, rubbing her arm. "Jesus returns to Capernaum, Lazarus! Come with us and hear Him for yourself," begged Mary. "He heals the sick, brother! He freed me of demons!"

Leaning in toward her brother, Martha added, "We have found favor with His followers, and have been invited to their home!"

Taking a deep breath, the skeptical brother looked at his sisters noticing their countenance. Turning to Sarah, he saw her pleading heart. *"Must I?"* he asked reluctantly. The women quieted when he suddenly asked, "When do we leave?"

Their hearts full, they cheered, embracing him. They filled their bellies with even more stone-baked fish and hot bread, pouring their warm wine, *again.*

Chapter Four

THIS SIDE OF MERCY

Mary of Magdala was well on the road to a strong, healthy life. The women who attended to the care and support of Jesus loved Mary and Martha very much. In Jerusalem, they gathered at the home of Jesus's Mother, to hear more of Mary's attack and help her heal. Under the sheltered wing of His Mother, Mary would learn as others did, to have a teachable spirit. Her transition to learning self-discipline was eased through her willing, eager-to-learn heart. Mary was excited about her *new life!*

The Mother of Jesus, her name Mary also, loved the Magdalene, enjoying all she learned of Mary's knowledge of oils, balms, and salts. Mother pondered in her heart the many things she knew of her Son and His purpose, remembering the Magi and their gifts of frankincense, myrrh, and spikenard presented to Him, at His birth.

Mary was braced with a keen understanding. Perception was a gift from God she did not know she had, holding these things precious, now. She learned the Lord's plan was weaving them together and how her talents and skills were helpful in the family of God.

With her knowledge of horticulture, Mary made balms and ointments for sale, often trading with perfumers and potters. She was taught well on the benefits of olive and almond oils, salts from the Great Himalayas brought by traders on the routes. The Fuller's Field, outside Jerusalem's gates, was a favored place for women, finding a wealth of minerals in the clay. Mary was known for her warm, earthy blends of myrrh, with its healing benefits.

When alone with the women, Mary would ask how it happened that she had demons. It troubled her not knowing what they were or understanding what it meant. "Why, *if I am the least* in my father's house would God want to free me?" she pressed. "I am a sinner, far from God. I stopped honoring Him long ago," she lamented. "Sinners are dedicated to the moon-god[4]. How can I be dedicated *back* to God, now?"

"No person is past the reach of God. He loves us, Mary. This is a grace that saves," added Susanna, a devout follower, healed by the Lord. Marveling at the simplicity of these wealthy, prestigious women, Mary's heart continued to soften, realizing their devotion to Jesus extended to her as His *daughter-disciple.*

"How is it that Jesus has the power to overcome devils? What does it mean to have devils? *What were these demons I had?*" Mary pressed. "Those devils had you!" said Salome standing. "The moon-god? Jesus has taught us *there is only One God!* Ignoring God's boundaries leads to sin and sinfulness, opens the door to devils."

"Tell her, *tell her!* I *try* to tell her!" Martha pleaded.

Joanna heard the desperate concern in her voice and drew close, "Mary, to love anything more than God is the sin of idolatry, even stubbornness. We've learned from Jesus that lies, lust, and demons rule perversions and work through our flesh and carnal nature, to keep us

---

4 www.biblebelievers.org.au/moongod

separate from God," she continued. "Only sin can keep us separate from God, most especially embracing sin."

Salome moved to sit next to Mary, saying, "Sin is an unclean devil and works through a person's speech and actions. Did you know that? Jesus <u>casts out</u> all devils! Mary, devils flee at the command of Jesus and the people are at once awakened and in their right mind!"

"We've seen Him drive out deaf and dumb spirits, even madness," Susanna shared. "These rule the minds and hearts of people, causing torment, sickness, even death!"

"We didn't get to see the demoniac near the Gadarenes turned loose, though," interrupted Salome. "What a miracle to see, that would have been! Pigs! *Can you imagine?*"

Joanna turned to Salome sharply, scolding, "Enough!" The room fell quiet at her tone.

Salome leaned in, embarrassed but determined, whispering, "They say multiple voices emerged at once when he spoke." She avoided Joanna's stare. "That's all," Salome ended, hiding her smirk.

"It is the power of God that overcomes the evil force of the devils and their every way of working," injected Mother. "It is far above the natural laws of this world. It is God with us, Mary. **HE** is God with us. There are many things you must see and learn *on your own* as you continue to learn from my Son. *Whatever* Jesus tells you to do, *do it* with all your heart, and you will see for yourself. You will *know* for yourself. The path to follow is that of the Lord. Stay close to Jesus," encouraged Mother reaching her hands out toward the eager disciple and bringing her near. She had a way of making one feel like a loved child again, regardless of their age.

The women who followed Jesus had adopted Mary into their family and shared many of the truths she had not already heard herself. They continued to share all they had learned and heard from Jesus. She was "like a sponge dipped into the love of God," Martha would often say. Hope was evident on Mary's face, as it was on the others, and joy!

"The Lord goes before us, Mary. There is *nothing* to fear," said Susanna. "His love for us has *no* boundaries. *Nothing* can separate us from Him once we are His. You will learn so much from Him, you will see," she reassured.

"I will continue to intercede for you Mary," Mother encouraged. "You *continue* to heal. Understanding of all these things is part of that. All is well, sweet Mary, you will see. Now, we must prepare for the travel! Many will attend the gathering on the hills." Turning to Mary and Martha, Mother smiled, "You're family now! You will join us, yes, and your brother?"

The sisters turned to each other, inspired by the strength of the women's ministry, and smiling with relief, chimed, "Oh, yes! Lazarus is coming!"

DAYS LATER

Crowds hurried through, racing toward the northern shores of the great Sea of Galilee, *early* in the morning. Near the hills, children chased and raced to find a spot close enough to see Him. Jesus was teaching that day near Capernaum and the people were hungry for more of His truth. Laughter filled the atmosphere and hope rose, shining brightly on the faces of the bound and the afflicted, even the lame *skipped* in their heart.

PETER'S HOUSE

Gathering at the home of Peter in Capernaum, the women rushed to gather much-needed supplies into bags. They too hurried to join the crowds toward the hillside. Mother was at the table while Salome and others went in and out preparing for the day's journey. Peter entered and smelled the morning's preparations of food while Mary and the women stuffed woven bags with food for the journey.

Entering, Mother, Joanna, and Susanna shouted with surprise, "Peter! You're back!" in near unison, happily greeting him with a humble kiss of brotherly love. The children present also rushed to embrace Peter, grateful and glad to see him. He was like an elder brother and providing protector to them all and often opened his home to the Lord and His family.

"This smells like such a happy place!" Peter laughed, rubbing his belly, kissing his mother-in-law, *now healed by the Lord,* and his wife. Looking around the room's hustle and bustle, he roughly placed a bag of freshly caught fish on the table. His eyes landed on Mary, who was kneading dough, attempting to ignore his boisterousness, when he noticed her fretting over something with her hands.

"It won't have time to rise," she flustered rushing to complete her task. "We have to be going."

Peter, hearing her fixed his eyes on her hands still kneading dough. "Veiny," stated Peter, matter-of-factly. "Very veiny."

Annoyed at the interruption and his forwardness, Mary looked up at him to see what he was referring to. Quickly realizing he was looking at her hands in the dough. *"Veiny?"* she blurted out, curiously annoyed at him.

"Yes, your hands are so strong your veins *pop* out," Peter laughed loudly. Grabbing dry bread and tearing off a big piece, he took a big bite. "You have veiny hands," he explained letting out an even louder, unexpected belly-laugh.

With resolve and slight embarrassment at the brash rudeness of his words in pointing to her strong hands, and still raw in her former nature, Mary turned to face him, stating confidently, "Your face is *veiny,* Peter." With her eyes on him, Mary firmly took a filled bag and slowing shoved it across the table. "And your *ears* are popping out! Here, go," she politely responded with a slightly crooked smile. "I am *Magdalene*," now standing upright and staring point-blank at him. A subtle reach for his right ear, Peter became aware his sarcasm did not humor her. Chewing the crusty bread-piece, some crumbling over his beard, his smile quickly faded.

"Yes, I know," still holding his ear. "Mary of Magdala, the *fish* tower." Taking the filled bag Peter quickly removed the crooked smile from his face. "Glad you're here. Taking this," he murmured looking into the bag of fresh bread. Turning to exit the house, he briskly joined the group outside, not knowing what to make of her.

Mary, letting out a sigh of relief, remained unimpressed. With much to do, she and the women gathered their belongings and followed. Soon the huge crowd swallowed her up on their way to hear Jesus.

CAPERNAUM

Children, joyful and full of excitement at the nearness of the Lord, filled the air with laughter. For the moment it was as if mischief was far and all agreed, celebrating life!

The cheering crowd continued to roar, "Our joy is full now! Our promised Messiah has come! Jesus of Nazareth! The son of a carpenter leads us to triumph over our oppressors! Jesus!"

Mary rushed past the group of cheerers and made her way to the front of the line where Lazarus was talking with Martha. Pressing through the cheerful crowd, she reached them, nearly breathless.

"Just passed this ravine and that slope, we should be right where the Lord is," Martha pointed out excitedly.

"Where have you been?" asked Lazarus, seeing Mary. "Trouble surrounds this Man, Mary. Don't be so quick to believe every prophet," warned Lazarus.

"It's such a beautifully inviting place." Ignoring him, Mary moved ahead toward Peter. "I will hear Him for myself," she said almost overwhelmed by the sea of people rushing toward Jesus. "I want to sit closer this time!"

"Again, I say! Turn the other cheek as well! Why foster a grudge?" Mary heard the voice of Jesus echo in the distance, preaching to the vast multitude of the sick and broken, *desperate* sea of people.

"Cheeks too!" she laughed.

"Not real cheeks," answered Peter. "He speaks of love over hate, not an insult for an insult, but bearing offense for the sake of peace, faith over fear."

"Fear?" interrupted Lazarus, riding up in time to hear the conversation, "I heard you feared and *sank*," he laughed. "Before that," replied Peter, "I walked on water!"

His words quickly got Mary's attention. "Sank? Walked on water? How?" she asked.

Turning to face her, Peter firmly testified, "I mean Jesus walked on water and called me to Himself! All was well until I feared and sank."

He smiled at the gawking Mary. "I'll tell you about it, another day!" he promised rushing ahead to help his mother-in-law off the cart.

Finding a shady spot, the group eagerly unloaded the carts. Peter helped his wife, John helped Mother. Mary rushed with Sarah, Joanna, Martha, and Susanna to set up a place to rest and receive from Jesus's life-changing truth.

A tattooed woman passing near them called out in a loud voice to Jesus, "Son of God, you've had mercy on me!" The woman and her daughter followed by a group of idol worshipers rushed toward the Lord. Jesus, hearing her cry, turned to see her.

"Who is this?" Mary asked Peter.

Peter smiled, looking her way, "Another one of Jesus's miracles, a Canaanite. An outcast one day, freed and belonging the next." Turning to face Mary he continued, "Jesus heals them all." Peter smiled walking toward the Lord who was greeting the Canaanite woman and meeting her daughter.

Suddenly an angry voice rose from the crowd addressing Jesus, "Pilate provokes us! Guards surrounded Jerusalem rushing through with banners! Caesar's image was hailed through our courts, Jesus! It is enough!"

Another voice called out in frustration, "We've heard You say You came not for peace but a sword; rise and lead us over our oppressors, Teacher!"

The mixed crowd grew more restless and confused. "What of the Galilean worshipers?" the zealot continued. "Slaughtered as they prayed! Their blood mixed with the blood of their sacrifices!"

Mother turned to Joanna. "Claudia," she whispered, "there was *more* that troubled her at the gathering in Bethsaida when she gave me the gifted scarf."

Jesus, listening patiently, stepped toward the angry zealots, "Do you think their sins to be worse because of how they died? I tell you all **if you do not repent** you will die just as they did. Tyre!" Turning to the Canaanite woman and her daughter He continued, "Bethsaida, Capernaum! The miracles you have seen and *still you will not fully turn!* Gomorrah will have it better than you *unless you repent!*"

"Mother," Mary leaned over asking discreetly, "what does repent mean?"

Mother turned to face her, smiling at her eagerness to know. "It means to feel and show remorse for sin or wrongdoing; to turn from the way of sin and unbelief, to the way of God." Taking Mary's hand gently, Mother pressed, "It is the *new life* shown by actions, not just words. Turning from all evil, Mary. It means to believe in God fully."

Mary turned to the Canaanite woman and her daughter meeting eye to eye.

"These were followers of the moon-god, Mary" Peter whispered in her ear. "Now they've turned to God because of Jesus and His love for them."

Time passed and Mary continued to work on adjusting her personality and self-willed spirit to learn humility with the women who served the Lord. Her reputation, stained from decades of self-indulgence and squandering of her family's wealth, had left a deep mark within her. The encounter with Jesus that dry, dusty day left her healed and delivered from the control and power of hateful men and of demons.

The strongholds of the world that had worked themselves to the core of who she was, had lost their hold by the power of deliverance found in Him that day. She remained conflicted about her struggles, though, and had many questions no one could answer.

Her new life was clear, but behind every tree and upon every slope, even during the preaching of sermons, stubborn lurers and pursuers continued to seek and distract Mary, attempting to get her back to her former self.

Relentless, harsh treatment and violent incidents against women caused Mary to burst out in defense of herself and those who struggled to keep their oppressors and abusers at bay. One day, was the worst.

Screaming murderous threats to fleeing bandits, Mary halted breathless and disheveled. A young girl ran up distraught and afraid, crying. "They appeared from the tree line. I was going for supplies," she wailed.

Mary took the girl by the shoulders, scolding, "Do not travel alone... ever!" Turning to see a family passing by, Mary pointed. "Draw near to the women there," directing the girl their way. The girl ran off, when a sudden quickening of the Holy Spirit sent a rush of cool warmth over Mary's body and her face softened, bowing her head. She knew Jesus was near, as the quick impulse of His presence was familiar to her.

With many of her faults still surfacing though, she struggled through the guilt of those many flaws, finding it hard to face Him sometimes.

She had not approached the Lord alone since the day He defended and forgave her. Until now, she had managed to maintain a safe distance at all the gatherings, keeping with the women, watching and learning away from the crowd. Jesus had kept His awareness of Mary near His heart, though, and lovingly allowed her to draw near on her own. Jesus was very keen to the most intimate and passionate thoughts Mary held about life and love.

Now, in the moment of her distress He came upon her swiftly, yet gently. Turning to face Him she braced herself, imagining she must explain. Her horrified realization at her filthiness against His pure radiant beauty sparked a quickened alertness within her, immediately causing her to look down and away, ashamed. She had nowhere to hide. It was His silent, understanding smile that invited her to trust Him. How could she not?

"Lord, I hate them!" not able to lie about her feelings, Mary confessed, bursting into tears. Distraught that He had seen the ugly truth hidden within her heart, she screamed, "They are everywhere who love evil." Overcome with emotion, Mary cried out, "I hate what they do, I hate what they are. I cannot love as You do Jesus." The words spilled from her lips, and she buried her shame-covered face in the bosom of the Lord, weeping from the depth of her soul. Anguished for the multiple women and girls who continued to fight for the simplest of things, no one to shield or defend them, Mary cried out to the Lord for justice. The face of the Lord revealed His compassion for her in her rage and heartache. Holding Mary even closer, Jesus calmed her to a soft sob, saying nothing, but holding her close.

Whispering, Jesus comforted the weeping woman, finally, saying, "There is nothing to be ashamed of Mary, nothing. No one knows My heart in this as you do. My Father's righteous indignation burns in you, as in Me, but <u>remember</u> My words: to hate is to kill, in the spirit of your heart. Hate kills, Mary." Mary, quieted by His voice, did not move from His hold, but clung even tighter to the Lord. Jesus calmly lifted her face to His.

The beauty of His radiant smile overcame her grief and frustration, softening the edges of her anguish. The gentleness of His beautiful hands framed her angry, distraught face. His fingers gently swept over her cheeks, wiping her tears away. Slowly, the reassuring words of the Master filled her heart, as Jesus lovingly stated, "Mary, this fierce love you have for Me and your passion for what is life and love will usher you through many hard and difficult places." He continued, firmly, "It is the very force that has brought you this far. Do not be so hard on yourself. Understand the signs of the times, and the purpose for which I have called you to witness these things. Even what it is to have anger for the right reason."

"Lord, they seem to be everywhere, those who embrace evil and those who cannot hear Your Words!" Mary erupted again, falling into His arms. He calmly hushed her, patiently and lovingly holding her close.

"More, as the days of our trouble draw near. All things work together for good to those who love Me," Jesus said taking her face in His hands.

She failed to realize the Lord was pointing toward His betrayal, arrest, and death. Mary turned her face away, embarrassed. "Lord you saw my anger; my hate."

Lifting her face to His he said, "I saw your love, Mary. Anger for the *right reason* is a sign of love, but yours *crosses over* to sin."

"I was furious! I wanted to harm him! The very thing you teach us *not to do,* I did! It wars *within* me," she cried with all her heart.

"That anger has its root in fear; it is an anger that kills. It is common to man. All must choose love over hate," Jesus reminded her.

Collecting herself, she recalled His many sermons on choosing love, forgiveness, and mercy over hate and a grudge or hardened heart. "You are always here for me, Lord. You never leave me; You never abandon me." She was overwhelmed with gratitude. "I have so many questions," she wept.

"Ask," Jesus quickly responded. "There is nothing you cannot ask," He encouraged.

Calming herself, Mary mustered the courage, "You walked on water? The waves carried You, Peter also. How?"

Jesus responded, "It was faith that called out to Me. I hear faith, Mary. Fear forced him under when his eyes veered off Me."

Mary looked long and hard at Jesus and mustered the courage. "What were those demons I had, Rabbi?" she finally asked.

"Those demons had you!" Jesus quickly replied.

"What does that *mean?*" she cried aloud again, not understanding what it meant to be *held* by a devil.

Jesus took her by the shoulders and stood her straight, looking at her. "The eyes are the way to the soul. You stopped looking to God, much like Peter taking His eyes off Me," He calmly stated. "Lust finds its way through want. Desire comes through lust. The lust of the eyes and flesh, the pride of life. Pride comes before the fall every time, Mary. Pride is the fall of man. It is the gate to every unclean thing," He further warned, urging her until He saw that she grasped His words.

"This war within me wakes when I wake and lasts through my sleep, Lord," Mary cried. "I try to do good. The things I hate *most* of myself, I end up doing the most! What is wrong with me, Jesus?" she wept aloud.

"Ah," He softly responded, "the war within. That war of yours will is a *daily* battle, a daily *choosing*. Let your choice be for life *and* love. All else is death, a curse. Follow love, Mary. Follow peace. Choose life. I came to give life. There is *nothing* wrong with you, *trust* Me."

Nearing the bend in the road, they had made their way back to the town's border. Her fears had all dispelled when she mustered the courage to ask what had been pressing on her heart since her first encounter with Him. "What were You writing on the ground, that day?" she cautiously inquired.

Recalling the day of her deliverance, He smiled, "The first time or the second?" He stopped and turned to look at her.

"Both!" she replied eagerly.

"What do you *think* I was writing?" He asked.

"Their names!" she blurted straightforwardly, causing Him to burst into laughter.

"It is written in the Prophets of old, 'Lord You are the Hope of Israel; all who forsake You will be put to shame. Those who turn away from You will have their names written in the dust because they have forsaken the Lord, the *spring* of living water.' You have been learning much, I am glad to hear! But no, not their names," He assured her.

"There is so much to know and learn," she replied, overwhelmed.

"Just know you are loved, Mary," Jesus smiled. "Again, what do you *think* I was writing?"

Pausing in her still newly rising confidence, her heart seemed to swell. "My name?" her hushed voice replied, a crooked smile warming her face.

Her head bowed, He turned her to Himself and in a sweep of joy, shouted, "Let it be according to your faith, woman!" He gleamed, laughing, kissing her forehead. "And *again*, there is *nothing* wrong with you, Mary!" He smiled. And with that, they rushed on into Bethany.

"And *no,* not your name," He chuckled.

MARY'S CRY

Mary loved the newness of life and the freshness that overtook her every sensation. It amazed her. The words of Jesus slowly stirred deep within her. His lessons fascinated her, working to heal and make her whole as she meditated on each word. Jesus knew very well her bruised condition, although her brokenness was not visible to others. He lovingly answered her every question, calming her every fear. Mary grew strong in the Lord.

He is like the balm of Gilead the older women speak of, whispered Mary within the quiet of her spirit. *He is ointment to my soul,* her thoughts agreeing with her heart. Mary made her way through the house, readjusting cushions for seating, as they had invited the Lord to come and refresh Himself and dine with friends and family at their home in Bethany.

Eager to learn, Mary understood the teachings of Jesus, helping others grasp His vast, dimensional, yet simple lessons. Many young women also gathered daily from smaller villages nearby as she encouraged them to draw to Jesus. Little did she realize she was already ministering to women and children. Mary encouraged and exhorted them, helping with simple truths. She learned about temperance, patience, and most of all diligence. The simplicity of Jesus's teachings helped her develop in the knowledge of God's love. She absorbed the Lord's lessons on humility, and how learning it can cure pride. Her greatest struggle was in *patience,* for wrath often provoked her when learning of the unjust, shameful treatment of women and girls in their region. Self-control of her thoughts was difficult, because of vengeful images *in her mind,* leaving her in tears and often worn.

BETHANY: HOUSE OF PRAYER

The home of Lazarus was dedicated to prayer and helping others. Jesus came to fellowship and encourage the people who gathered and preparations for feeding them were well underway.

The Lord enjoyed the love and atmosphere of this home, a favorite place to retreat from the demands of the day and His journeys to the Temple in Jerusalem, daily. It was a place where He could rest, surrounded by family and friends.

Martha, overtaken by the details in preparing for her guest, was meticulous about every detail. Managing to *over manage,* she grew annoyed, stirring a boiling pot of fish soup over a blazing fire. Steam covered her sweaty, fuming face when Lazarus walked in following the aroma. He heard her flustered, and corrected her, saying, "Calm yourself, Martha! It's only Jesus, not Caesar."

Turning to face her brother, surprised at his words, Martha caught herself, *held her tongue* and instead replied, "Brother, I love you. Go. Sit!" And with that she rushed him out the door to greet the Lord.

"Good fish soup," he called back, mischievously.

Frustrated with her sister's lack of helpful service to her in the kitchen in preparing for so many people, Martha was flushed, faint, and flustered. Mary could not peel herself away from hearing Jesus teach, though. She learned to pay attention and absorb all He taught to those who hungered for more; she was the hungriest of them all.

"No Better Place" Inspired by Northernway

"It would be much appreciated a little help in here!" Martha called out flustered. Fretting to herself she hustled and bustled to produce a meal fit for a King!

"She is consumed with the teaching and not nearly aware of all your fuss," Susanna pointed out and helped all she could, herself. "Her hunger is for the words of Jesus, Martha, look at her face!"

"Lord!" hollered Martha. "Don't You care? My sister has left me to do all this work *by myself!* Tell her to help me!" She foolishly assumed she could direct His hand, selfishly implying He did not care.

Jesus smiled. "Martha, cease from all your hard labor. A simple meal is more than enough. Mary has chosen a much better portion and is doing well by it," He said pointing out Mary's eagerness to learn.

Quickened by His response, Martha minimized her tasks in order to not miss what was left of His teaching. She motioned for Susanna who quickly took over her place, allowing her to sit for a while and let the words of Jesus refresh her. Suddenly, as she moved to sit near her sister, Martha realized the love Mary had for the very words He spoke. The captivated Mary could not take her eyes off Him. How He loved the people, how He healed the sick, His Words raising them from beds of suffering. It was as if she had known Him *all her life.* It was as if she owed Him *all her love.*

"How do I know I'm forgiven?" Mary openly asked Jesus, suddenly. "Not all agree, Rabbi. The pharisees do not approve, still; the people whisper as I pass," she poured out, tearfully.

Turning to address her heart's cry, Jesus looked directly at her. "Your forgiveness does not depend on the approval of others. You are forgiven and delivered, Mary. You must choose to accept it for yourself," He urged. Reaching to touch her hand, He smiled. "It is a gift from God freely given."

"Rabbi, I find Your words to have the power to change a man's heart," Lazarus added. "My sister is a changed woman. I am sensing change as well," he continued turning to the gathered villagers. "We all do." Jesus was glad to hear Lazarus and the assurance in his voice, once doubtful, and so was Mary.

"I believe I understand," Lazarus continued. "When You say we are forgiven by *faith* but I don't know what it means when You say, 'you must be born *again.*'"

Jesus, happy to hear such inquiring, stood and said to the crowd, "Many find it to be a difficult thing to imagine." Turning to Lazarus He said, "Your heart and mind must be renewed from all that is old. The old is corrupt and dead. What we receive from God by our trust and faith in Him is the *new life* with its *new law of love.*"

Turning to Mary then Martha, Lazarus finally admitted, "Then it *must* be true. I *must* be born again. Let the journey begin!" he laughed full of joy.

The remaining fellowship was joyous and awe-inspiring, the hearts of God's people content. The day had been a full one and the hearts of the people fully enjoyed the presence of the Lord.

"There *always* remains a desire for more," smiled Lazarus, greeting his guest's goodbye. None could know it would be the *last time* they would see Lazarus until the day of his resurrection.

"These departures are always *more* painstaking," Martha agreed, holding her brother near. "I've learned *so much* tonight, my brother," she whispered, tired but refreshed by the wonderful fellowship of friends. "Our sister loves the Lord *so very much.* It's His *very words* that she cannot seem to get enough of. I can *see those words* illuminate her heart, *almost.* I cannot explain it." Lazarus, comforted by her observation agreed, embracing his *much*-loved sister.

Their love for each other, as a *family,* had grown and flourished and their lives transformed gradually from within, as the words of Jesus's teachings were taken to heart. The words spoken by the Lord had a life all their own and had already grown *roots* in the hearts, minds, and lives of the new disciples. They would be forever changed.

As night fell and all retreated to their homes, a quick silence came over them all. Hurrying to be alone with the Lord in the meditations of their heart, they would soon see greater demonstrations of the power of God more personally, more *intimately.*

"His Words are healing to my bones," Mary prayed, settling that truth within herself. "His words," she whispered, "are *healing* to my bones!" radiating sweet, glowing knowledge. *"His words take root within me,"* she smiled. Their sleep was sweet that night, and all was well in the world.

71

DEATH of LAZARUS
Winter 32 A.D.

An unusually, bitterly cold, winter swept through the region with fierce force, not like other winters. Many children and elders fell ill as hope for a short season had long left their minds.

"Where is He, Mary?" wept the feverishly weak Lazarus, enduring a long illness they could not relieve. *"Why* hasn't He come?" he lamented in pain.

Mary wiped his brow and giving him drink, softly replied, "He has never lied, brother, nor will He delay. He will come. Rest now," she reassured, trying to comfort him as much as possible.

Lazarus worsened and grew gravely ill, not able to recuperate. Waking early in the morning, Martha found her brother burning of fever and struggling to breathe, he was dying. By nightfall, the sisters, overcome with grief, were struck by the sudden death of their brother, and desperately sent for Jesus, saying *"Lord, he whom You love is dead!"*

Failing to hear from Him after two days, their heartache and sorrow worsened. Harsh rumors spread about Jesus not caring for the family or the death of Lazarus, among the gathering mourners. Some even quoted His recent words, *"Let the dead bury the dead."* But Mary and Martha remained in prayer, waiting with fading hope.

Bursting into the home, Sarah quickly realized the heaviness that lingered and calmly approached Martha, who was folding away Lazarus's clothes and coverings. "We've sent for Him, again," she whispered to Martha.

"He won't come. The crowds keep Him, and the cold. It's been days," Martha grieved. Staring out the window at the morning light, Mary responded in a daze, "Four days. It's been four days. For two days it has not been so cold," she tearfully pointed out, not looking their way.

Perplexed by the continued delays and seeming detours to any explanation, now four days after his death, Lazarus had putrefied. The sisters questioned between themselves and came to reason that Jesus was hard-pressed by the needs of so many others. Struggling to make peace with those thoughts, they held out their faith in prayer for the Lord's soon return.

Mindful of the Lord's promises, meditating on His every word and recalling His every healing move, Mary wept again. His mercy had always been great, superseding *any* hope imagined. Mary *still* struggled to trust.

Nearing Bethany on the fourth day after the death of His friend, many people were on the path and greeted Jesus, for Lazarus was much loved and was very well-known. The sisters heard of Jesus drawing near and Martha hurried to meet Him. Mary remained in the home, *mourning,* on her knees, in prayer, attended to by Sarah and the elder women from the village.

"If You had been here, my brother would *not* have died," Martha cried falling into His arms. "But I know, *even in this,* the Father will not withhold the request of Your lips, Lord." Looking into His face she continued, "Whatever You ask from God, He will give You."

Taking her face in His hands Jesus reassured her, "Your brother will rise again, Martha."

Overcome with grief Martha cried, "I know, in the resurrection on the last day."

Calmly embracing her as she poured out her heart to Him, Martha was reassured of the Lord's ability, hoping in His willingness against all the odds. Her great faith in Him prompted a burst of overwhelming energy, as He declared with a passion not noticed by her before, "I AM the Resurrection and the Life! Those who believe in Me *will live* even though they die, and those lives who have believed in Me will never die. Do you believe this?"

"Yes, Lord, I believe that You are Messiah, the Son of God, who is to come into the world." Her trembling faith burst forth her confession of who she knew Him to be.

"Where is Mary?" He asked.

"I will call her for You, Lord," lovingly kissing His hand, she turned rushing for Mary who remained waiting for Him. Bursting through the door Martha yelled, "He's here and calling for you!" Jumping to her feet Mary ran to meet Jesus, others racing behind.

When she saw Jesus, falling to His feet, she cried, "Lord, if You had been here, my brother would not have *died!"* Seeing her so broken and weeping Jesus's heart was heavier and deeply troubled, moved to tears. He turned to the mourners who comforted them, saying, "Where have you laid him?"

In near unison, the mourners replied, "Lord, come and see," pointing and leading the way. Jesus wept.

Many complained and grumbled saying, "Could not He who opened the eyes of the blind man also have kept this man from dying?" Grieved and deeply moved again, Jesus drew near the tomb seeing it was a cave with a stone laid against it and stood, not saying a word. Mourners canvassed the hillside of the cave while others moved in closer.

"ROLL AWAY THE STONE!" came the Voice of the Lord, thundering suddenly *through* the unsuspecting mourners.

"Lord, by this time the smell is extraordinarily strong and foul! My brother has been dead for four whole days!" reminded Martha, desperately. "Did I not tell you," Jesus responded calmly, "if you believed you would see the glory of God?"

Martha motioned the strong men standing by, and they collected themselves closely together, positioning and bracing themselves to roll away the mammoth-sized stone. With great, unified force and effort, the strong men leveraged themselves as one. The boulder, after much force and effort, gained traction, resting its weight in the cave's crevice.

"Father, I thank You for hearing Me," Jesus prayed aloud. "I know You always hear Me but I say this on account of the people standing here, that they may believe that *You* sent Me."

With those words a sweet, *yet still,* atmosphere came over the area and a tangible presence descended over the people. An unseen weight of warmth swept over them all, and they distinctly heard a faint sound emanating from within the cave, an indescribable movement, a vibration.

"LAZARUS COME OUT!" roared the voice of the Lord, demanding and *specifically calling* out the one dead man. Other deceased loved ones that had been laid to rest in the large cave also and may have risen, had the Lord not called out Lazarus alone.

A faint glow gradually increased, emanating from the mouth of the cave deep within. Unexpectedly, what sounded like a *brush* of angels' wings, a soft wind, gently exhaled over the crowd. A sound of hushed excitement swept over them, moving *through* them. Many who were spread a little farther out quickly moved closer, some leaning on each other nearer the cave's entrance. In awe, they witnessed a ray of light radiating through.

RESURRECTION OF LAZARUS

Immediately a *shuffling* sound, thumps, and drags came from the entrance of the tomb as a woman in the crowd let out a shocked scream! A shadowy figure could be seen moving, *wrapped and bound,* catching a ray of light, breaking through the darkness. The gasps of the people, some near fainting, rushed through the crowd of mourners now witnessing the glory of God. The angels of the Lord all around, none seeing their splendor, were there to witness in absolute wonder, the mercy of our God and the power of the love of Jesus. God's Holy Spirit was there.

None could speak for the richness of the glory overshadowed them all with a weighty substance none could see, but only feel, when suddenly there emerged the wrapped body of a man. Bound with linen strips at his hands and feet, his face wrapped with a tight cloth, Lazarus stood trying to maintain his balance. Mary, with arms stretched toward the body of her disoriented brother, stood breathless. Martha, falling to her knees, held herself and sat. Tears filled her eyes.

"UNBIND HIM AND LET HIM GO!" came the commanding authority of God through the mouth of His Son, Jesus.

The full authority of God over death had uttered its voice through the Lord. Death bowed its knees in rehearsal for the great day of His own Resurrection. His victory over death was now demonstrated far before He would ever hang on the cross. Raising to life a man He would soon Himself die for, ultimately to raise Himself from death by the Holy Spirit of God, Jesus stood triumphant.

Rushing forth, the men who had rolled away the stone obeyed Jesus, knowing they were witnessing the glory of God. The wraps were removed firmly. Some were pulled and others supernaturally fell off as Lazarus emerged clean and purely radiant, full of life.

His eyes struggled to adjust to the glory of God and the newness of life radiating all around them. He was fully encapsulated in the visible, touchable glory and presence of God. Awestruck in wonderful amazement, the people lifted their voices to the heavens praising God. In the distance, a few were seen running toward the city's entrance to spread the news.

"Jesus had raised Lazarus from the dead! Lazarus was ALIVE!" "LAZARUS LIVES!" one shouted, entering Bethany. A crowd quickly gathered and others rushed toward the tomb. "LAZARUS son of Cyrus, LIVES!" They rushed to tell all they had seen.

The Lord loved Mary so much and was so moved by the faith of Martha that a glorious light hovered all around them.

"Lazarus, you're... *alive!*" Martha uttered. Her frozen smile slowly absorbed the joyful warmth of life before her, touching him gently, feeling his face.

Mary clung hard to the hem of His garment, overwhelmed by the mercy of His love and compassion for her brother, for them. Her gratitude spilled through her tears as her mind tried to grasp and comprehend the fullness of what had just happened. Life had swallowed up death, right before her eyes. He who was once dead, **now lived!**

The resurrection of Lazarus did more than wake him from the dead, it woke a sleeping giant within the evil hearts of those who opposed the Lord. From a distance, those who had set their minds to plot against Jesus looked at each other with rage. Seeing the joy of the miracle before them, celebrated by those who loved Him most, infuriated the haters of Jesus.

"We meet with Caiaphas, now!" seethed Simon. "He will challenge this Jesus." Scarcely able to refrain or hide the visible traces of his disdain, Simon quickly slipped away to further strengthen the alliance of those who were leading the revolt against the Lord, His method, and message.

Disputing Pharisees and Sadducees surrounded a big, stone-like throne chair where the current High Priest sat. Caiaphas, leader of the plot against Jesus, ridiculed the slothful priests, fuming, "You lazy priests know nothing!"

Perplexed and hesitant but determined, the Sadducees whined back, "He is raising the dead! If we let this radical continue, everyone will believe in Him!" Facing removal, they continued working feverishly to persuade the evil ruler, saying, "Rome will come and *remove us* from our place and our nation... and *you!*" they warned the High Priest, aloud.

Standing to his feet, glaring directly at them, Caiaphas seethed, "Think! Jesus is one man. It is better for *one to die for all* than for all to perish for one." Turning his back to them all, he added, "Jesus is the *one.*"

Abruptly entering, and staunchly approaching Caiaphas, Simon rushed in. "What is it now? Jesus, I'm sure," retorted the High Priest. Simon leaned to whisper in his ear. The enraged Caiaphas led the treacherous Pharisee toward a veiled wall and handed Simon a filled leather coin-bag as Judas stormed in, rushing past the conspiring Sadducees. Seeing Judas, Caiaphas removed himself, swiftly and discreetly behind the veil to watch.

"Feet swift to shed innocent blood, an *abomination* to the Lord," scoffed Simon to Judas. "What brings you?"

Judas, sweaty and disheveled, paused to catch his breath. "What has Caiaphas ordered?" he finally asked. Reaching into his breast pocket, Simon retrieved the pouch he gained from Caiaphas and showed it to Judas. Snatching the bag with a smirk, Judas's face turned pale gray, as death marked his now lost soul.

Late that night, alone with her thoughts, Mary remembered the Lord. "How can I not fully trust Him?" she argued within herself. All that He demonstrated in mercy and compassion, in both patience and in understanding her eyes could not deny. The Lord had filled the void, wordless places within her with His word, reaching her and bringing her to life. Shameful places and experiences had suddenly lost their painful hold. Lustful thoughts, she wrestled and warred with, further shaming her, she now realized she had not struggled with for some time! Mary had experienced the touch of a new life!

Her mind renewed, her hope alive, Mary whispered as her eyes closed for the night. "I'm ALIVE, too!" she smiled at the goodness of Jesus for Lazarus. With hardly a sound, Mary fell soundly to sleep.

SPRING 33 A.D.

Bethany buzzed with rumors of strife and contention among religious leaders, convinced that Jesus must be stopped at any cost. Their alliance was strengthened by their jealous fear, coupled with their covetous deceptions over the people, and so were driven forcefully onward.

Soon, it was just days before Passover and many events continued to unfold with debate, excitement, curiosity, fear, and wonder all surrounding Jesus. The raising of Lazarus and cleansing of lepers caused divided uproars among the people, most for fear.

Preparing at the home of Lazarus, Martha shared the news with Mary of the invitation to Jesus, his disciples, and friends, to sup with Simon the Pharisee. The *father* of Judas Iscariot, among many others, pressed hard to be near Jesus lately. Mary knew very well the invitation did not extend to her. It was her fierce love for Jesus that fueled her well beyond the borders of her shameful past, though. She, too, had been a leper of sorts, as an unclean sinner. "The Pharisee? He loathes me!" Mary fumed in disbelief. "He insists I am not forgiven and am worthy of stoning, *still!*" Mary choked back her tears and mustered her confession aloud, "I admit I looked at the man with desire. I admit he returned the same to me. It was so long ago! Does that call for my death by stoning? Why is mercy only found with the Lord?" she cried aloud.

"Mary!" Martha interrupted. "Lower your voice!"

But Mary was already stirred and pained by this and continued pressing hard against this partiality and injustice. "Jesus said I'm forgiven! Am I or am I *not?* He said hate *kills!*" she wept. "The crowd calls Jesus a trickster," Mary poured out, unrelenting "and I believe Simon is behind it!"

"If a priest declares a leper clean, I can be clean as well!" she argued tearfully, speaking up for herself for the very first time.

"Mary! Jesus is not a priest!" Martha whispered loudly, standing to her feet.

"He's *my* Priest!" Mary cried aloud, not holding back.

Sarah, rushed to her side to help calm her, saying, "I'll stay with you, Mary."

Adamant about the hypocrisy behind her treatment, Mary let out, "Jesus teaches there are no differences! Clean is clean! Somebody is lying!" She stormed out of the room alone, sobbing and deeply hurt.

The room falling silent. Hearing Mary sobbing, through the door Martha finally spoke softly, "I must leave soon, Sarah. Mary will be fine."

Refusing to heed the voice of shameful ridicule and belittling insignificance, Mary *warned away* the force of evil intimidation that came to weigh her down. She was *far* too grateful to let *anyone* stop her.

Mary moved quietly in her room, taking two wooden wash bowls, a square reflective tin, and her ash-colored dress. She took the tin in her trembling hands and looked at her reflection sadly, whispering to herself, "You too have been unclean. You've lied. You've cheated and cursed."

Looking away tearfully, Mary finally admitted to herself, whispering, "I have hate in my heart." Laying down the tin, Mary took the bowls and filled them with water, preparing to wash.

She let down her long-braided hair, undoing it gently and rested her feet in the cool water. Shortly after finishing her preparations, and wearing her nicest, simple, woven ash-colored dress, Mary quietly took the beautiful vessel and climbed through the lattice window.

Quickly sneaking to the front of her home, she took a lit torch and rushed toward the setting sun. Through the quickly approaching night, Mary dared not arrive with the others. None were aware of what

the Lord had put on her heart to do. With stealth and precision, Mary cut through the night and made her way to Jesus. This *woman on a mission* could not be stopped.

Shielded with a fierce love for Jesus, she would soon walk past all her enemies straight up to Him, ministering to His most pressing need, to find an answer to *her* most pressing question, "Am I truly forgiven?"

As evening settled, the festive sound of fellowship could be heard coming from within the home of Simon, the closer she got. The known leper healed by the Lord continued to make himself *preferred*, among others. From a safe distance, the undeterred Mary could see through the lattice Martha, Joanna, and Susanna happily preparing the meal.

ANOINTING JESUS
Saturday

Holding herself at the door's entrance, the costly nard in her trembling hands, Mary slowly moved toward Jesus. No one noticed her except the Lord and Judas. The Lord, aware of her every move and step, turned His attention to Simon who loathed her very presence. Jesus knew the thoughts of all and turned back to look at Mary.

Not having mustered up the courage to hold her head up in such a prestigious setting in so long and knowing it was not a place for a woman of her repute, Mary moved past her paralyzing fear. Her only mission was to reach the Master. As if being carried on the wings of the wind, she moved toward her Lord as He watched her faith in Him emerge. Jesus was aware of her every breath.

With every move, another betrayer was silenced as Mary took each step-in-time. One by one, heads turned as the invited guests soon realized it was Mary, and she did not belong. With the alabaster flask safely nestled at her bosom, she firmly cradled the beautiful carved-stone vessel. Knowing it must make it to the feet of her Lord, she determined each step accurately with stealth and precision, closing the gap of time. Soon, the *beginning of the end* for all her abusers, accusers, and users would start.

Mary held the oil, a costly ointment of genuine nard used specifically to anoint the Lord for this moment. That which would anoint the Priest and King, held and carried by her, reached through rays of opulence as if reaching for the Lord. The oil remained guarded in the costly translucent alabaster flask near her heart.

Making her way through to Him, Mary now stood behind Jesus at His feet, nervously grasping the vessel at the neck too tightly, accidentally breaking the flask. Unnerved, she tried gently pouring a bit of oil at the crown of His head to anoint Him, when a gush streamed out, spilling and dripping over His ear and neck, embarrassing her. The oil ran down Jesus's face and beard. The despising Simon, forgetting his own former uncleanness, leaned toward his son Judas to his left, and whispered, "Surely if this was a prophet, He would scarcely allow Himself to be touched by a sinner, much less a *wom—*"

"Simon!" interrupted Jesus startling him, "I have something to say to you."

"Say it, Teacher," Simon quickly turned.

Mary continued wiping the abundance of oil that overflowed now, nearing His feet, and seeping to the floor. She carefully made sure her hair only touched His feet, drying them again and again, as her tears spilled forth. Mary was overcome with appreciation and gratitude for Jesus.

Turning His eyes to Judas, Jesus directed His question to Simon. "A certain moneylender had two debtors," began the Lord. "One owed five hundred denarii and the other fifty." Now, looking Simon's way, Jesus continued, "When they could not pay what they owed, he canceled the debt of *both*. Which of them will love him more?"

Surprised and facing humiliation, Simon answered, "The one I suppose, with the larger debt."

Jesus returned, "You have judged correctly."

Mary, not able to lift her face, wept. All in the room witnessed the pouring of her whole soul into this one act of love. No one knew the depths of despair of which Jesus had rescued her from. She alone knew how vast and wide the gulf that swallowed her up in guilt was. It had suffocated the life from her very hope. Her sins were many. She could never repay the debt of forgiveness she had received from Jesus, nor explain the love that resulted from that very act.

Drying her tears and His feet with her hair, Jesus continued, turning to look at her. "Do you see this woman?" He pointed to Mary, bowed overconsumed in her worship of Him.

Weeping and unmoved, she tried to remain discreet, overcome by the beauty of the Lord before her. Taking her hair, she carefully dried her falling tears. Her mouth, once used to curse and to damn so often, speaking proud and lofty things and debating against anyone who hurt her or those she loved, now kissed the feet of her Rescuing Redeemer.

"You invited Me to your house," Jesus pointed out looking directly at Simon. "But failed to welcome Me, giving Me *no water* for My feet." Now turning to see Mary, Jesus continued, "This woman has not ceased washing My feet with her very tears and wiping them with her own hair. You gave Me *no kiss*, but from the time she came in, she has not been able to cease kissing My feet. You *failed* to anoint My head with oil, but she has anointed My feet with rare, costly ointment. This is the reason her *many* sins are forgiven." He turned, looking at each man present. "She loved much." Turning again to face Simon, Jesus made Himself clear, "But he who is forgiven little, loves little."

Turning His attention to her, Jesus took Mary's face in His hands and lifted it to see into her eyes once covetous, now consumed with love for Him. Gently He smiled to her saying, "Your sins are forgiven, Mary." The brightness of His eyes fully reflected His love for her.

She would be the last person He would forgive face to face before the horrors of His cross. Mary smiled back and closed her eyes, a tear running down her cheek. The Lord brushed back the hair from her face and declared to all present, "I tell you, wherever this Gospel is preached throughout the world, what Mary has done will also be told in memory of her."

After anointing Jesus, Mary withdrew stealthily, cautiously cleaning the area around her. Slowly, as she retreated, she noticed the piercing gaze of those who despised her presence. The mixed disciples whispered, "Who is this who even forgives sins?"

Jesus was very aware of Mary and the words being whispered about Him, and so called out to her aloud, "Your faith has saved you, Mary. Go in peace!"

Lifting her head, assured of His love and forgiveness, Mary quickly bowed it again when her eyes met His, "Thank you, Jesus," she smiled and turned to leave the room.

She could not have known these would be the last words her Lord would ever speak to her, face to face. She would never hear His voice echo through the valleys or soar to the hilltops of the beautiful region, nor see Him walk the shores of Galilee, again. She who would preach the powerful Resurrection saying, "I have seen the Lord!" would see Him no more. Mary quietly turned and walked away into the dark of night alone, holding her broken alabaster flask to her heart.

Immediately, a wave of discontent filled the room as there were some who did not agree with the intrusion, becoming indignant and murmuring amongst themselves, instigated by Judas. Grumbling his discontent louder and louder, Judas stirred himself to wrath. Slamming his hand on the table, Judas stood fast and raised his voice, questioning, "Why was this fragrant oil wasted like this? It might have *sold* for over three hundred denarii and," stalling to think of some reason, "given to the poor!" he criticized sharply. He cared nothing for the poor, avoiding many opportunities to bless them.

Jesus, moved with frustration at Judas's continual critique of Mary and instead fixed on her loving act, defended her again, saying, "Let her alone! Why do you continue to trouble this woman? She has done a good work for Me. You always have the *poor* near and *whenever* you wish you may do them good. Me, you will not always have. She has done all she could, coming early to anoint My body for burial and with her whole heart."

Disturbance mounted as the guests were both curious and perplexed. Divided amongst themselves, some nodded and whispered their agreement with the Lord, while others remained unsure. None fully understood what Jesus was *truly saying* about Himself, nor what was about to take place.

As supper ended, the household servants removed the last of the table scraps and bowls. The devil had fully persuaded Judas to betray Jesus. **The next day**, being Sunday, Jesus entered Jerusalem cheered and celebrated by the Passover crowds that gathered for the great event crying out, "Hosanna! Hosanna in the Highest," waving palm branches toward the heavens. Everyone knew who He was. This further fueled the fury of the priests and Sanhedrin who rushed on the balcony to hear what all the commotion was about.

"They cheer as if *He* were God," one old, snarky Sanhedrin official complained, looking down on Jesus riding a young colt.

"His days are numbered," replied another. "The son of Simon comes often to us, Judas!" he gloated with a smirk.

"Yes, the son of the Pharisee; he serves us well," murmured the old official now looking at Mary and the women who followed Jesus.

"These women," pointed the old priest, "why are they so dedicated? And the Magdalene?" he said eyeing her with disdain as she gladly celebrated Jesus and agreed with the shouts of the growing crowd.

"His supporters," replied the official, scornfully. "The Magdalene had devils, they say," he chuckled.

"Supporters?" snapped the old man, "How? In what way?" he demanded.

The priest turned to the old man with a smirk, and with an air of mockery, replied, "Paying Caesar what is his, and from the heart," he laughed. "Give God what is His: tithes, land, offerings."

Sneering, the old man turned quick, "Untaxed? This explains *why* the son of Simon comes. Is he not the money handler for this Jesus?" he smirked, watching Mary. "Gifts from the heart to God?" he snickered, "just like a woman." Jesus, looking from the gate, saw them, knowing their thoughts.

Early the following morning on Monday, the crowded city prepared for Passover. Peddlers of doves and lambs, spotted and black, hurriedly placed them on old dry, rickety tables throughout for people to pick through.

Entering the courtyard, the disciples and Peter saw the compromise and chaos of the frustrated people picking through doves and lambs not finding any that were suitable. Jesus, followed by Mary and the women who served Him, entered. Quickly, seeing the cheap and blemished animals where those to be offered to God should be, Jesus stormed the tables flipping everything in His way. He turned over the tables of moneychangers rebuking the hypocrisy and disregard of the merchants. What was not thrown was scattered, of the sick and lame offerings. There were none found to be useful enough to present to God as a sacrifice and Jesus could not bear it.

"This place is a house of prayer!" He roared, enraged, like never before. "You thieves bring scraps and rubbish to God!" Jesus stormed, going through every table, tossing every blemished thing in His fury.

Peter and the disciples pushed the women out and Mary turned with Peter to look through a crack in the gate, astonished.

"Hypocrites!" Peter angrily slammed his hand on the gate.

Jesus could be heard yelling at the top of His voice, "This is the house of God!" Animals scattered; women screamed.

Turning to him, Mary asked with concern, "Peter, what do we do?" At a loss for words, he could only shake his head. Rushing out the gates of the city, Jesus bolted past Peter, Mary, and the others. Looking at Mary, Peter quickly followed an angry Jesus. He had held His peace for so long. Jesus's time had come.

THE LAST COMMUNION
Thursday

It was the first day of the Festival of Unleavened Bread upon which the Passover lamb would be sacrificed. Jesus instructed the disciples where to go to prepare for the meal, as they had inquired.

Directing Peter and John, He instructed, "Go into the city to a certain man and tell him, 'The Teacher says: My time is near. I will celebrate the Passover with My disciples at your house.'"

Following the instructions of the Lord, Peter and John set out to make the preparations. As they entered the city, an old man with a watering jug met them near the gate and led them to the house where they inquired of the master of the house, who led them to an upper room already set.

The day was exceptionally long and overexerting as the women busied themselves with the details of where the Lord would sup. It was a solemn assembly He had called for, asking specifically that the Twelve alone commune with Him for this supper.

Finishing the preparations for the evening's supper, the women quietly withdrew to Mother's home in the city to break bread and pray through the night. For them, it was simply another time to gather, with no hint of what *or who* waited for Jesus. The approaching Passover was on every family's mind, *as on theirs,* and it was a beautiful night.

"It is good that men meet alone with Him," Mary said. "More often the women need to come alone together and encourage each other, as well."

Mother sat near a stone-fire warming herself. "I am glad we have time to ourselves. It's important as women to come away and help bear each other's burden, lighten each other's load for a bit. I have much to share," she divulged softly, rubbing her tired feet. "Passover is near," she smiled.

"Mother," asked Salome, "please tell us of Jesus, of when He was a child." Her face gleamed with excitement to know all she could of Him. They shared bread and meat brought from the home where the Lord and His disciples were for the night and sat around to hear as Mother shared fond memories of Jesus as a boy. As she shared, she recalled each detail of a marked event. She told of when *Jesus* was lost.

"Every year we journeyed for days to Jerusalem for the Festival of Passover," she began. "He was only twelve years of age when we attended one year, as we had customarily done. This journey, while returning home, we realized He was not with us. He was not with anyone! We failed to realize Jesus had stayed behind in Jerusalem not informing anyone! We were an entire day's journey away when we saw He was not among us. Not until three days later we found Him in the temple courts sitting among the teachers, asking questions, and teaching what He knew. Annas was High Priest, then."

"Did His questions provoke the elders?" smiled Joanna adjusting herself on the bed-cushions.

"No, on the contrary!" Mother beamed. "Gladly, it amazed everyone who heard Him. His understanding and His answers were intriguing, although not all were glad."

"What did He say when you found Him?" asked Susanna.

"I couldn't believe He would treat us like He had," chuckled Mother. "Causing Joseph and me much worry, but all He did was *question us* for not already knowing He would be where we found Him, as He said, 'In His Father's house.' No one could know what we know now, nor understand those sayings."

The peaceful tone of shared, fond memories and laughter was just what the women needed. Their thoughts were quickly comforted by the stories of Jesus as a young boy, wise for His age and fearless. The bond between the women continued to flourish and strengthen, growing in trust, in confidence, and prayerful support.

At the home where the disciples gathered with Jesus, He quietly observed their fellowship, listening closely to their conversation. John alone noticed His solemn countenance. Jesus reclined with the Twelve as evening came. The sound of peaceful joy filled the room where they rested from the long day. Quietly reminiscing, they shared the marvelous signs and wonders they had been so privileged to witness.

The Lord quietly absorbed their every word when without warning He leaned forward declaring, "Truly I tell you, one of you will betray Me tonight." The room fell silent.

Saddened and heart-struck, the disciples repeated their disbelief at His words one after the other.

"Surely You don't mean me, Lord?" Peter asked right away.

John, seated next to Jesus, leaned his head on the Lord's breast instantly saddened at the thought and whispered, "Who Lord?"

"The one who dips his hand into the bowl with Me will betray Me," Jesus answered. "The Son of Man will go just as it is written about Him. But *woe* to that man who betrays the Son of Man! It would be better for him if he had not been born."

Then Judas, the one who would betray Him, looked straight at Jesus, saying, "Surely, not *me*, Rabbi?"

Jesus looked directly at Judas. "You have said so," the Lord answered the betrayer, dipping the morsel and giving it to his hand, already in the bowl. Jesus, then, leaned in very close to Judas, face to face, and whispered, "What you are about to do, do quickly." Judas squirmed.

Restlessly, he adjusted himself at his seat, writhing in his guilt. The Lord's piercing gaze cut straight through him. As the tense conversation shifted, John drew nearer to the Lord seeing Jesus had grown increasingly troubled. John turned to see an evil shift in the eyes of Judas.

Staring back at the Lord and overcome by evil, vengeful anger, Judas tried to hide his shameful hate. Turning, he abruptly left the room as the bread and cup of juice passed on to the faithful disciples, and before anyone other than John and Jesus could notice.

Looking on, Jesus watched Judas scurry to do evil. John, speechless, leaned the whole weight of his body over on the Lord burying his face and wept, the Lord hushing him with a comforting embrace.

While they were eating, Jesus took bread and when He had given thanks, He broke it and gave it to the disciples, His friends, saying, "Take and eat; this is My body," passing it to them solemnly. Then taking the cup, Jesus lifted it the same and when He had given thanks, He turned and gave it to them, saying, "Drink from it, all of you. This is My Blood of the covenant, poured out for many for the forgiveness of sins. I tell you I will not drink from this fruit of the vine from now on until that day when I drink it new with you, in my Father's kingdom."

Finishing their last supper together, the disciples that remained rose together and gathered their belongings to depart. One by one they approached the Lord to show their love and appreciation. Embracing Him, they quietly exited the upper room for the last time, together.

Passing through the Essene Gate near the Fuller's Field, closest to the upper room, they made their way along the wall near the Pool of Siloam. None spoke along the winding route when a song, a traditional hymn, rose softly in the distance, gradually growing louder. Families could be heard celebrating and preparing late into the night for the festive meal that was to come. The sound of joy and laughter could be heard.

As they passed the Golden Gate nearest the temple, herds of lambs *unusually calm on this odd night* were led through, innocent of what lay ahead, as priests prepared to receive them for the slaughter.

Jesus watched and prayed.

It was the eve of the Passover. The disciples, less one betrayer, followed the Lord. Making their way past the walls of the great city, through the winding, dirt-rock path, they began their ascent retreating to the press of oil near the Mount of Olives, for the night had fully come.

Judas rushed, breathless and sweating toward the temple, and the priests who waited. Through village roads to the secret gathering place of the plotters, he ran single-mindedly to finalize plans on how to arrest the Lord.

Chapter Six

HIS ARREST & DEATH
Near Midnight, Early Friday

THE MOUNT OF OLIVES

Peter brought firewood. John stoked the small blaze. "It is written," Jesus said, shattering the silence. "Strike the shepherd, the sheep will scatter; you will all fall away, tonight."

Peter stopped in his tracks stunned at His words, dropping the logs near John, blurting out, "These will. Not me!" he boasted pointing to the disciples.

Standing to face him, Jesus cautioned leaning in closely, "You, Peter, will deny me three times before the cock crows twice."

Peter's countenance turned gray. "I would die first than deny you, Jesus!" he replied taking Jesus firmly by the shoulders.

Holding His gaze on the face of His prideful disciple, Jesus responded, "Keep alert, Peter. Pray." With urgency in His eyes Jesus continued, "The tempter comes without a word." Turning up a higher hill, Jesus withdrew to be alone. Halting, He turned to the men, saying once more, "Watch and pray."

MOTHER'S HOME

Awake at the window, Mary stayed peering through the lattice, listening. She faced the shadowy path as if expecting someone to approach. Her eyes drifted their search toward the moon-filled nightscape. *Pressing in* to hear something not clear, she prayed, sensing the prompting of the Holy Spirit. Leaning in to hear something far away, Mary was unaware of the angels of the Lord that held watch over those who love Jesus. They were not visible to the naked eye. Hearing voices rise in the night, Mary peered harder through the window seeing several torches and guards, then Judas.

Her right palm over her heart held the broken piece of alabaster tight. Holding it against her breast, her thoughts were on the events of the previous night. Mary recalled how the Lord reassured her forgiveness, leaving her with no doubts. She prayed through her troubled thoughts of those who despised her, trying not to wake anyone. In another room, a young girl wept, tossing in her sleep.

THE MOUNT OF OLIVES

Just outside the borders of the village, confrontation stirred. Disciples in disarray scrambled to hide, some positioned themselves to defend the Lord. Guards led by Cassius, the Commander of the Guard, ascended the foot of the hill when Andrew saw them. Torches in hand, the guards marched toward Jesus. Andrew raced to wake Peter. In the shadows, others scurried to find a hiding place or way of escape. Peter pulled his sword at the abruptness that woke him, standing to his feet.

Andrew pulled him down low, informing him of what was fast developing. "Down, Peter, look!" Andrew warned, turning Peter toward Jesus. Peter ran to Jesus, sword in hand, leaving his brother mid-sentence.

Making his way through the trees, Peter's eyes fell on Judas. Through the shadowlike dance of firelight flickering through the forest,

Peter witnessed Judas lead the way to Jesus, escorted by a company of guards, followed by a crowd of on-looking rabble. Peter's eyes, fixed on the face of Judas, tightened the grip on his sword, racing to Jesus's defense. Jesus waited.

MOTHER'S HOME

The calm night grew balmy and a little windier as Mary paced through the house, not wanting to stir anyone. The child, disturbed from her weeping, rose to find Mary awake. Shaken from a bad dream, the girl whispered rubbing her eyes, "I dreamed of soldiers and fire." Mary rushed to comfort the child when suddenly, the young girl said in fear, "Who has taken the Lord?"

Startled by the words of the young girl, Mary assured her it was just a bad dream and settled her back to bed gently. "No one has the power to take our Lord anywhere against His will." She smiled as she tucked the girl in and leaned to kiss her cheek, lifting the coverings to her shoulders. Brushing the child's hair back, Mary tucked a rag doll near the small girl's heart. "Here you go, take this," she said warming it to her cheek playfully. "Remember, Jesus loves you very much." She then kissed the girl's forehead. Leaning up, Mary turned her attention toward the door, again, as if someone were coming. She recalled the attempt on the life of Jesus, when the crowd tried to push Him off the cliff and He walked right through, untouched and unseen by any of them.

"They couldn't kill Him then," she whispered, turning to the sleeping girl. "They cannot kill Him now. *No man* takes His life."

THE ARREST

Peter approached the Lord swiftly, running up with his sword by his side and halted fast. Guards stood *on defense* as Peter neared, causing the tension to thicken. Jesus calmly stood watching while confusion swirled all around. None were aware of the thickened evil that loomed. **"Who are you looking for?"** Jesus demanded loudly with eyes of fire, standing calm.

In supernatural array and not visible to those gathered, angels stood shoulder to shoulder waiting one word from Jesus. A retorted snarl of devilish hate came from the guard with an evil grin, "Jesus the Nazarene!"

Subtle changes in facial expressions among the arresting guards swept over them as the evil in them slowly emerged, showing its face through theirs. They could not hide or contain their appetite for evil, not realizing it was the seed of their father, *the devil,* working in them.

"I AM HE," was the clear blast of truth that pierced through the dark evil that came to say *He was not.* His eyes fell on Judas, who stood trying to hide behind them. The power of His words thrust all who were standing against Him backwards and to the ground, stunning them hard. Again, He asked, **"Who is it you want?"**

A snarl of gritty evil came, "Jesus the Nazarene." Judas emerged from behind Malchus, the ear-boy to Caiaphas.

"I told you, **I AM HE.'** If you are looking for Me, then let these men go," Jesus said when Judas approached, kissing Him on the cheek. Peter, suddenly and without warning, swung swift and hard with great force, cutting off completely, and in one stroke, the right ear of Malchus. Chaos ensued and time stood still. Blood gushed from his wound, as Malchus clutched his head, faint. With blood pouring down, soaking his garment, Malchus wobbled to his knees, pale, as death drew near to devour him. With a word the Lord commanded calm, turning to Peter, "Put your sword away! Shall I not drink the cup My Father has given Me?" His voice rose over the chaos. "If you live by the sword, you will die by the sword!"

Reaching to pick up the severed ear, Jesus put it back on the bleeding servant, bowed over in shock. Sudden warmth numbed the pain as the kneeling Jesus covered the place of the wound. A bright light flashed just beneath His hand, subtle yet quick, as the flesh of each piece reached to connect themselves to each other. Supernaturally, the place of the cut closed and the blood dried in its place. Malchus was healed.

"You'll be alright," assured the Lord, love for the man radiating through Him.

Now horrified and in shocked disbelief, Malchus reached his trembling bloody hand to touch where the ear miraculously attached. His eyes fixed on Jesus and in stunned disbelief, he whispered, "My King."

With sudden brutal force the detachment of guards, observed by Jewish officials standing at a distance, arrested Jesus. Jerking Him violently to His feet and binding Him tight, they deliberately hurt Him. Judas swiftly ran ahead of the chaos just as Cassius stepped forward ordering, "To Annas!"

Pulling and pushing Jesus, shackled at His feet, hands and neck, the brutal Roman guards mercilessly overtook Him and hauled Him into the dark to the former High Priest and father-in-law of Caiaphas, Annas.

With only the dancing of flames left shadowing off the trees of the forest, torches faded into the night with the sound of rabble left to dissipate.

Jesus remained silent, not resisting the guards who pushed and jerked Him all the way to the High Priest's chambers.

Peter fought his way free from those who tried to arrest him, running into the darkness toward the Lord's captors, followed by another disciple. Only a few remained with Andrew, Matthew, and John. Others ran, hiding behind trees and boulders, watching as Jesus was taken, chained.

Helpless and terrified, the confused disciples saw one guard after another push and mistreat the Lord. Jesus did nothing to defend Himself. The crowd rushed off toward the city, closely behind those who had arrested Jesus. The light that once danced among the trees, their flickered shock, faded to darkness and Malchus stood alone, weeping.

"It has begun," whispered the grief-struck John in disbelief. He turned to face his brother disciples who all stood speechless and afraid, then rushed for Mother and Mary through the dark, followed by a few.

Panic filled the roads as news of Jesus's arrest raced through the city and region. The sounds of chaos filled the streets as people rushed through spreading the news and choosing sides. The voice of strife and debate grew louder and louder, the echo of voices rose to the heavens. The people, scattering in panic, were divided, confused, and alarmed.

Peter arrived discreetly, at the gate nearest Caiaphas's court. Seeing the crowd grow restless, he moved to warm himself by a small fire, farthest from the priests.

A servant-girl walking through the yard noticed him trying to conceal himself and thought he looked familiar. Determined to know, she turned to him, asking directly, "You aren't one of this Man's disciples, are you? The Man, Jesus?"

Immediately and without hesitation Peter snapped at her sharply, **"No, I am not!"** and walked away briskly to warm himself by *another fire* when the sound of the cock crowed loud.

MOTHER'S HOME

Mary rushed through her home grabbing a flask of water and a broken loaf of bread nearly falling over herself, not knowing where to turn. No one was prepared for what the thief in the night came to do.

She hastened to gather with those who had come with Andrew and John, along with the disciples, to tell of Judas and Jesus. Mary spun around, making her way to the door, rushing behind Mother. Without warning, Mother halted as if something or someone had stopped her.

Lowering her head to gather herself, she turned to Mary and strengthened her stand. "There is nothing we can do, Mary," Mother whispered, taking Mary's face in her hands and looking deeply into her terrified teary eyes. The desperate, frantic look of despair quickly came and settled over Mary's face as she refrained from her collapse.

Tearfully she whispered, holding back her terror, "They cannot take Him against His will. God will **not allow** it, Mother, please!" Mary was fighting back the tears welling and filling up in her frightened eyes.

"I know what you say is true, Mary." Mother sighed, the heartache in her voice, trembling. "It is *also* true the will of God is that we witness and tell all," she said her eyes filling with tears. A glow of peace surrounded her, seeming to infuse her with strength. A faint smile traced her lips.

There has always remained a sense of knowing with Mother. She held so much in her heart from the start of her journey with Jesus.

Turning to all in the room, she declared boldly, "That we experience and testify to what is about to occur, did He not tell us and has He not well prepared us? How often has He pressed us to know this time would come? Did we believe Him? If so, now is the time to show Him. Now is the time to stand with Him, Mary?" Her gaze now turned to her most solemnly. "You *must* be strong."

Mary, overcome with grief and struck with dismay, fell into her loving arms. Together they crumbled to the floor grievously overcome. Mother of our Lord held Mary close to her heart, cradling her with much love, praying softly.

An Angel of the Lord moved toward the women, who could not be seen. Only a strong sense of urgency overcame them.

"Jesus is calling us, Mary. He has need of us and we must not delay," wept Mother, pulling Mary up along with herself to their feet. They wiped each other's tears and braced themselves for what lay ahead.

John pressed the women. "They've taken Him to Annas?" he said looking at Mother and opening the door. Turning, they rushed out, making their way through the overshadowing and wickedly dark early morning hour.

Standing by a second fire, Peter warmed himself again. Others had noticed him and wanted to settle a small dispute amongst them. They turned to him and asked, "You aren't one of His disciples too, are you?"

Startled by their abruptness, Peter quickly looked up aggressively blurting back, **"No! I am not one of His!"**

Not completely convinced, one servant, a relative of Malchus's, challenged him further. Drawing slowly toward Peter and sure he had recognized him, he came up behind him, saying, "Didn't I see you with Jesus at the garden? I am sure of it, the man who cuts off ears!"

Peter, agitated by the imposing closeness of this man, turned to face his accuser sternly declaring, "I am **not the man**!" The cock's shrill crow, piercing Peter's soul, sounded in the distance. Alarmed and struck, as if by death itself, Peter withdrew running into the night afraid and ashamed, deeply struck by grief. Peter was alone.

ANNAS

The frenzied crowd filled the courtyard outside the house of Annas. The former High Priest was father-in-law to Caiaphas, who hated Jesus and led the plot against Him.

Annas, annoyed and sleepy from being awakened in the middle of the night, called for help. A servant assisted him to a cold throne-like seat. Guards entered with Jesus abruptly. Joanna, Mary, Mother, John, and Andrew entered discreetly in time to hear Annas yell out over the crowd, "Who have you brought to me, and at this hour? What is the crime?" Turning to Jesus, visibly shaken and already beat, Annas tried to see His face clearly, through his gray and aging eyes.

Frustrated and grumpy, Annas snarled to a silent Jesus, "What is Your crime?" Peering through his clouded eyes, Annas leaned closer, glaring at the Lord. "I know You... Jesus, the Teacher of teachers," smirked the old priest. "Apparently, Your message is more than a message to some!"

Looking to Annas, Jesus replied, "I have said nothing wrong. All who have heard Me know that to be true."

A guard struck hard at the head of Jesus nearly knocking Him down. "Stand down, Jew," he ordered, slapping the Lord, again.

Sleep deprived and unamused, the yawning Annas waved his hand. "Take Him to Caiaphas," he ordered wobbly rising from his throne and motioning for his servants.

"He is High Priest now. I have heard enough," the old man murmured, turning and shuffling away.

With that, they led Jesus like a lamb to the slaughter, saying not a word. The guards dragged Him violently, scribes and elders murmured with content as Mary helplessly watched Jesus being dragged out. Turning to Mother and John, Mary rushed out toward the courts of Caiaphas.

CAIAPHAS'S COURT

Debate erupted through every road and home, from villagers to the religious elite. All rushed to the courts of Caiaphas, many led by Simon. John led Mary and Mother, pushing through the angry crowd when Mary noticed Peter sitting discreetly, blindly watching Caiaphas stare at a disheveled, already bruised and scratched-up Jesus.

Two false witnesses stepped forward to accuse the Lord. One raised his voice over the chaotic crowd, "This man said He has the power to destroy the Temple of God!" The room fell silent.

The other raised his voice, "And to rebuild it in *three* days!" The two men looked at each other sheepishly just as Caiaphas rushed toward Jesus, screaming aloud, "I order You in the name of the living God, answer me! Are you the Messiah? A king?"

Jesus lifted His eyes and gazed at the profusely sweating priest. Mary held her breath. All held their breath as the room shushed to an even more piercing quiet when Jesus responded, "You said it yourself. You will see Me sitting at God's right hand, coming on the clouds of heaven."

Tearing his garments in half and screaming as loud as he could, the *enraged* High Priest yelled in the faces of the gathered religious groups, "Blasphemy! You heard it yourselves! What more do you need?"

Scribes and elders responded quickly in one hot breath, "Death! He deserves death!" Many were tearing their garments in a rage and circling Jesus as one hot mob.

In nearly *one sweep* of motion, violent guards overtook the Lord. The merciless guards spat at, kicked, and blindfolded Jesus. They mocked Him, bowing to Him sarcastically chanting, "Prophesy! Who hit You? Was it me? Was it him? Prophesy, prophet! Where are You? Why are You here?"

Peter could barely stand to watch, turning his face and sneaking out as the ruthless guards slapped Jesus to the floor. Mary and Mother, shocked speechless, could not look away. John watched in stunned disbelief, pulling the women out of the room, not able to take his eyes off the Lord. The bloody, silent Jesus was beaten. The drooling Caiaphas, enraged to the point of spitting, ordered, "To Pilate!" And the mob overtook Him again.

In grievous disbelief and now in hiding, Peter woke briefly as the morning dew struggled to welcome the light. A faint flicker danced off the cave walls where he had retreated. A small fire burned. The haunting, echoing of taunts from those who had recognized him filled his mind with despair and torment. Again, he recalled the words of the Lord and the wailing crow of the roosters' scratchy alarm.

Withdrawn and afraid, confused and in isolation, Peter mourned the Lord. With great beads of sweat falling from his head and face, he agonized, broken, on the dusty floor of the cave. What he had done had no explanation. Bouncing off the walls of the cave where he had found a place to crawl, just outside the borders of the city, Peter remembered the water. He remembered the voice of Jesus beckoning him and walking toward the Lord. Then the third sound of the cock's crow echoed through his soul, again, and suddenly Peter recalled the words and face of Jesus, saying, "The tempter comes without a word. Watch and pray."

The truth of Jesus's words worsened Peter's guilty shame. He had denied knowing Jesus. The weight of that guilt overwhelmed him, and he mourned uncontrollably, penitent and broken. Peter could not find comfort.

PILATE

The light of early morning arrived on the face of Pilate, angered at the sight of a beaten, bloody Jesus, tried without justice. The shouts of the rabble grew louder, threatening to riot, as both Mary's pushed their way through the pressing crowd. John was by their side with Andrew and others near, though further hidden by the crowd. So, Pilate came out to address their insolent anger asking, "What charges are you bringing against this Man?" knowing who Jesus was, and not holding the same staunch stand of his blood-thirsty fellow peers.

Exasperated, yet trying to hide their full rage, the rabble yelled back, "If He were not a criminal, we would not hand Him over to you." Pilate roared, "Take Him yourselves and judge Him by your own law!" "We have no right to execute anyone," objected the priests, not wanting blood on their hands, for they were guilty of falsely accusing Jesus. Execute?" responded Pilate agitated. "There will be a riot!" Turning to examine Jesus, Pilate desired to distance himself from this trouble and decided almost immediately. "He is Galilean. This is Herod's affair. Take Him! Go, now!" And thus, he retreated to his chambers abruptly.

Tossed back and forth, they removed Jesus without regard for His bloody and bruised body. Mary and Mother saw Claudia standing just out of view. Their eyes met briefly when Claudia looked away, weeping.

HEROD

The youngest son of Herod the Great, *Herod Antipas,* was ruthless and perverse. The Tetrarch of Galilee, *Rome's appointed king of the Jews by Emperor Augustus[5],* had long waited to be in the company of Jesus. Pacing through rushed, Herod circled Jesus gleefully. "Finally! The Galilean... or, is it the Nazarene?" He smirked with a chuckle, exciting himself, alone.

Joanna entered from through a curtained doorway, followed closely by Mary, Mother and John. The room was strangely quiet as many odd and perverse, debauched revelers and servants stood around and watched *the one king* measure up the other. Herod scowled at Jesus, examining Him up and down, critiquing Him, abhorrent of His appearance. "They say You perform miracles; some say, signs from the heavens!" Herod taunted, leaning in closer. "What can You do for me?" He approached with a dry, cracked whisper. "I need a miracle."

Jesus looked at Herod through swollen eyes, struggling to stand. Herod's counselors flanked the ruler swiftly and two false accusers leaned in to speak, their eyes filled with hate for Jesus; they had been paid.

"Your father the Great Herod called for the deaths of infants thought to be sons of David," one craggy-faced counselor whispered. "The people call this one son of David: *King* of the Jews!" The old counselor despised the presence of the Lord.

"Rightful heir to your throne," another old man of the counselors interjected. "What would your father do now?" Jesus remained silent, bleeding profusely.

Herod, standing behind Jesus, recalled the great day of slaughtered innocent ones. He pierced through Jesus with his eyes, perplexed. Mary leaned in to hear the evil ruler speak. "How is it You

---

5 www.bibleodyssey.org/en/people/main-articles/herod-the-great

are here?" Herod inquired, snaking himself around to face Jesus directly. "Perform Your miracles now," he smiled, maliciously.

The silence of Jesus infuriated Herod who motioned for his guards to beat Him even more severely. All Mary and those who loved Him could do was watch, nearly faint. John blocked the women's view, but they pushed to see past him. As quickly as he raised it, Herod lowered his hand strangely satisfied, and the cruel punishment stopped. Jesus lay on the ground.

A wicked grin spread across the face of the evil ruler. Standing to get a better look at the Lord, he shouted, "Return him to Pilate! He's ordered to keep the peace! All I see is a bleeding man." The guards grabbed Jesus, yanked and pushed Him out of the court without another word. The chaos of the rabble roared louder and louder.

PILATE

Returning to the inner chamber of his courts, Pilate stood silent, his eyes fastened on the Lord. Now, on the grounds of Fort Antonia, Jesus faced the mixed crowd, alone. His body bruised and bloody, His head hung lower and lower as the cheers from his haters reached heaven, cutting deeper than any guard's blow. Pilate had heard enough and quickly grew flustered by the relentless, unjust accusations of the rabble, led and provoked by the priests and rulers, namely Simon. Herod's cunning move to return Jesus forced the final *verdict and fate* of the Lord to rest on Pilate, alone.

The strength and might of the unruly crowds intensified, forcing Pilate to motion his guards. Savagely, they grabbed Jesus and yanked Him to stand before the inflexible, cruel judge. Gazing intently at the Lord, Pilate inquired of Him, "Are You the King of the Jews?"

Looking directly at Pilate, Jesus responded without hesitation, "Is that your question or one you've heard?"

106

"Am I a Jew?" stormed Pilate, turning his back on Jesus, ranting. "Your very own people and priests' hand You over to me! What is it You have done?" Sitting himself down on the judge's seat he roared, "Tell me!" Jesus answered, without a flinch, "My Kingdom is not of this world. If it were, My servants would fight to prevent My arrest. My Kingdom is from another place."

Angrily addressing Jesus Pilate stamped back, "So, You *are* a King?"

"You say I am," Jesus responded, calmly. "I was born to testify to the Truth. All who side with Truth listen to Me," He continued when He saw Claudia emerge from behind the columns, handing a messenger a note. Horrified at Jesus, Claudia turned away only to see Mary and Mother watching her from the midst of the repulsive crowd and bowed her head, mournful and ashamed. She retreated behind the veiled curtains into the shadows, the messenger handing the note to Pilate. Examining the note himself, Pilate quietly read:

"This is a Holy man; dismiss Him. Do not condemn Him.
My dreams have spoken and trouble me, terribly."

Pilate crumbled the note, tossing it. Turning briefly to see Claudia, he noticed her weeping and watching Jesus. "What is the Truth?" he retorted sarcastically. Turning to the Jews gathered outside the courts, he declared loudly, "I find no cause for a charge against Him! It is your custom to have released to you *one prisoner* at the time of the Passover. Do you choose the King of the Jews?"

Shouting back in what sounded like one voice, they roared, "No! Not Him! Give us Barabbas! We want Barabbas!" The crowd in unison cried out, cold-heartedly, "Release Barabbas!" Cheering for the release of the barbaric heathen, the onlookers yelled in a cluster. Desiring the release of the murderer over Jesus, they yelled, "We want him! He is one of us!" The vile man had led past uprisings, and they knew him well.

Mother, held closely by Mary and flanked by John with Andrew drawing nearer, shared their shock at the appearance of the Lord. The murderous calls from the frenzied rabble rose to a near riot. "Who are these people? Why are they so treacherous?" cried Mary. "What has happened to them? I saw the Lord heal many of them!" she languished, dispirited. She had seen them on the hills listening to His teachings, partaking in the harvests of food miraculously provided for, so often. Jesus saw them, also, and this too grieved His heart.

"Look at Him!" replied Mother, gazing at her Son, "His eyes are on us." Looking away from the evil, double-minded crowd, Mary gazed on Jesus. "He wants us to remember everything," she whispered.

John leaned in to hear her, slowly nodding, "We must not leave His side. He is trusting us with all of this." Tears filled his eyes.

The push from the crowd intensified as did the hurls of sharp and painfully false accusations. "Blasphemer! Save Yourself! Perform Your miracles now!" they scoffed in their madness, hurling insults to the One Who formerly comforted and encouraged them.

"Jesus! Free Yourself," others cried. Flanked and provoked by zealots, partisans and religious leaders, the venomous rabble roared louder. Several of the disciples who had run, scattering at His arrest, drew nearer, shrouding their full appearances for fear of the growing unrest. They remained untouched in the safe distance, watching Jesus suffer. The more faithful followers stood alone, as near as they could to Him.

No one though could discern the evil, demonic spirits hovering all around, as if watching a sport. The Angels of the Lord flanked nearby awaited any Word from Jesus to quickly end all His suffering. One word from Him would have stopped everything. All hate and the evil, bloody death He would soon face for us all would have ended abruptly, had the Lord uttered His voice for Himself. But for the joy set before Him He endured, continuing to finish His divine assignment from His Father.

Children stood in confusion and dismay. Many wailed uncontrollably, some peered from behind the old stone walls, looking on in hopeless disbelief at the cruelty of the Lord's unjust punishment. Trying to comfort each other, one child reached out for Him.

"Jesus, I love you, please!" strained the heartfelt cry of Josiah. Pushing his way through the chaos, an adult grabbed him, saying, "Stop!"

Pilate motioned his officials who took the Lord by force and had Him flogged. The guards whose twisted and demented minds of evil and torture, which was their sport often, now twisted a crown of thorns and pressed it onto His head, piercing Him. Great beads of blood poured over His face. Taking a purple, ragged robe, dirty and torn, they clothed Him, taunting Him to His bloody face, repeatedly and without mercy. Pushing Him amongst themselves, they threw the tired, bleeding Jesus onto each other viciously, dizzying Him to no end.

Slapping His face, they repeatedly hailed, bowing in mocked sport, "Hail, King of the Jews! Hail, King of the Jews!" Forcefully grabbing, with the force of evil hate, one hand reached out and took hold of the beard on His face and pulled so hard it ripped off the flesh and the hair. The bloody and suffering Jesus struggled to stand, saying not a word. Violently, the guards took Him again and hauled Him off to Pilate.

Pilate returned to the gathered Jews saying, "Look! I am bringing Him out to you; I find no basis for a charge against Him." Then Jesus was brought out before them wearing the crown of thorns, robed in purple and covered in blood. Pilate, *horrified* at the appearance of the Lord, held his staunch position, and turning to them all, said, **"Here!"** pointing to our bleeding Lord, **"Here is the Man!"**

As the eyes of the priests fell on Jesus, they chanted in one voice, "Now, crucify Him! Crucify! Crucify! Crucify!"

"You crucify Him!" yelled Pilate over the riotous crowd. "I find no cause, no basis or reason to charge Him with *any* wrong!" he insisted.

Pushing back harder, the Jewish leaders retorted, "We have a law and according to that law **He must die** for claiming to be the Son of God!" Hearing this caused great fear to come over Pilate and he returned to question Jesus again. "Where do You come from?" This time Jesus did not respond. "Do You refuse to speak to me?" Pilate asked concerned, staring at Jesus's bloody stand. "Don't You realize I have the power to free You or to crucify You?"

Looking up to face him, barely able to see, Jesus replied, "You would have no power over Me if it were not given to you from above. Therefore, the one who handed me over to you is guiltier of a greater sin." The threats from the priests increased even louder, relentlessly against Pilate who tried to set Jesus free to no avail. Jewish leaders now shouted, "If you let this man go, you are NO FRIEND OF CAESAR! Anyone who claims to be a king **opposes** Caesar!" The noise of the crowd grew deafening and Pilate raised his hand for silence. As the last of the shushing murmurs came to a calm, the sound of bleating lambs rose in the close distance following their shepherds to the slaughter. The time for the temple priests had come for ceremonial sacrificing and preparation.

It was the day of the Preparation of the Passover and nearly noon when Pilate raised his voice over the hateful mob, "Here is your King."

They replied to his grief, "Take Him! Take Him away! Crucify Him, now!" Desperately concealing as much as he could of his severe disapproval of these events and their choice,

Pilate pressed the feverish crowd once more. "Shall I crucify your King?" he yelled over their chants.

"We have no king but Caesar!" came the staunch voice of the hateful Pharisee. With those words the people roared their approving agreement and Pilate made his final motion to those in command. Without warning, flanks of Roman guards appeared from both sides of the court's steps quickly surrounding the stage where Pilate, Jesus and now Barabbas stood. The forceful brilliance of the guards flanking shoulder to shoulder caused a dreaded silence to fall over the crowd all at once, now seized with alarm.

The crowd fixed their eyes on Pilate's every move except those who love Jesus. They could not look away from Him who loved them so. His appearance nearly beyond recognition, His eyes set on His Mother, the beautiful Mary could only weep.

Her eyes fixed on her Son with only tears left to speak of her grief. Mother whispered as Jesus turned her way, once more. "I love you," she formed the words as Jesus stood front and center. Soldiers on the other side had also grabbed, with much difficulty, Barabbas, who was violent, insolent and foul mouthed. Coming face to face for the first time, nearly touching, the evil eyes of Barabbas fell on the bloody Jesus. With confusion and loss on his face, Barabbas was quickly turned toward the chaotic crowd. Jesus also faced the people who shuffled for a closer view of this horrific tragedy.

Pilate motioned young boys, palace slaves, who rushed with a towel and bowl, the other a water pitcher. A hush fell over the rabble who struggled to be still, anxious as a drooling wolf. Satan's appetite worked through their blind unbelief. Taking the hand towel, Pilate dried and turned his back to the mob, still silent. With a wave of his hand, they took away the Lord. By force, the ruthless soldiers took Jesus for final punishment and scourging, to the wailing grief and shock of many who loved Him.

This would be the most severe, most mutilating assault any human would ever suffer. They beat Him beyond recognition for what we ourselves had done, for what we have always done. They would torture Him for our sins. There was no other way. There would never be another opportunity for humanity to enter heaven, except for the ultimate sacrifice made by Jesus, a punishment and death of unimaginable proportions. God the Father would soon turn His face away from His only begotten Son, Jesus, as He Himself *became* sin for us replacing *our punishment* and death with *Himself.*

The suffering Lord carried His own cross through the mixed chaos of people, many wailing along the painful way. The ruddy route lined with lovers and haters alike would reach the entire length of His journey. The path lined with mockers, betrayers, and hirelings of the uprisings made against Him, looked on in strange contentment. Without warning, a guard grabbed a bystander, a witness named Simeon, placing the full weight of the bloody cross over and on him. Jesus could go no farther. Those who love Him pushed their way through, helping Him as they could with drink, wiping His brow and kissing His face in absolute disbelief and shock. The blood-soaked Jesus saw Mary through the crowd trying to reach Him, but quickly turned His look away.

GOLGOTHA

The place of the skull was the place of His piercing. With callous disregard guards forced the Lord to the ground, the dirt covering and filling His every open wound.

On each side of Jesus, others were being nailed and raised. He soon would hang between them. He would soon hang between the worlds. Mercilessly, they placed Him on the raw, fresh-cut wood beam. In the temple, the priests, also, hung the lambs.

Slamming the weight of the iron hammers to the nails with fierce ferocity, they pierced Jesus's hand in one blow, as if to extract the fullness of breath from the Lord's body. He gasped in frozen shock, the pain rushing throughout the core of His being. The second arm, grabbed by heartless men, was pierced and fastened with force.

Snatching His bloody feet, they too were nailed to the beam, piercing the Lord with great force and without mercy, finishing the violent act of nailing Jesus to the cross. Callously, one guard took the sign ordered by Pilate written in Aramaic, Latin, and Greek. Reading 'JESUS OF NAZARETH, THE KING OF THE JEWS.' He fastened it to the wood beam over the head of the Lord. Despite the harsh protests from the priests and Sadducees, Pilate ordered it so, saying, *"What I have written, I have written."* It was custom to post over the head of a criminal, their crime and reason for execution. Pilate sarcastically complied with their demand and strove to maintain their custom, as they desperately forced on Jesus. This further highlighted their guilt, further increasing their shame.

Mary stood as near to the foot of the cross as she could. Jesus was slowly dying before her, unrecognizable. Helpless, her hands that once anointed His head and feet reached for Him as darkness quickly overtook the brightness of the noonday. The sun grieved. A very dark, thick fog obscured the sun and the moon. Stars barely flickered, trying to see from their heavenly abode, three men on three crosses on top of a hill. An empty, hollow feeling descended on the people, perplexed, some wailing while nearby guards, not waiting for death to finish, took His clothes and divided them into four, one for each of them. Only His fine linen undergarment remained: a seamless, one-piece tunic woven from top to bottom. They greedily admired the beautiful, expensive fabric yelling, "Don't tear this one! We can decide by lot who will get it!"

The thick evil surrounding them, rested gladly on them. As if in a trance, those who looked on stood frozen in time.

Mary, nearly faint, looked on horrified and appalled when two guards on horseback, one with a spear, drew near to the foot of the cross, poking around the Lord's feet. Horrified, the women rushed to surround Mother, retreating her to safety. Mary never took her eyes off Jesus.

He was still breathing. The full weight of His limp body hung loosely from the restraints that bound Him from the horrific assaults He had endured. His pale face, gaunt and hollowed, his eyes sunken, the Lord lifted His parched, blood-dried face to the heavens, gasping in prayer. No one was able to discern His words. The pain was beyond excruciating.

His body, struggling to be still, jerked with tremors and chills. Blood flowed from the gashed, swollen wounds that covered the Savior, collecting at the foot of the cross, dripping slowly from His beautiful feet and toes.

Simon, the shamelessly foolish religious leader, approached the foot of the cross like a coward, scoffing, "How can You destroy the temple and build it up again in three days?" Turning to the crowd of shocked onlookers Simon continued, "He always wanted to help others, and He cannot even help Himself!" Watching Jesus die, Simon coldly asked Him, "Are You the Son of God? Then, come down from the cross!"

Turning to the mourners Simon provoked them further, asking, "Is He the King of Israel? Then let Him come down from the cross and we will ALL believe Him! He trusted in God." Simon turned to face the Lord and looking directly at Jesus said, "Let God help Him now! For He said, I Am the Son of God!" Simon and the others jeered relentlessly. The Lord, silently dying, watched him.

Hearing and seeing the heartless Pharisee, John secured Mother from the vicious, hateful words, consoling her. With them stood other women and Mary. Jesus saw her reaching for Him, weeping.

Turning His face away He saw, also, His mother and John and called to her, "Woman... here is your son."

Tearfully, He turned to John, setting His eyes full of love, saying, "Here is your mother." Now, the many obvious fulfillments of the Scripture escaped them all still, yet knowing everything was nearing their Divine completion, the source of all Life and waterer of souls turned His head saying in a dry whisper, as if to Himself, "I am thirsty."

Then Cassius on horseback dipped a spongy, rag-tipped spear into the bitterly raw concoction of wine-vinegar. The stench repelled those nearby. Now spoiled and foul, he soaked the sponge putting it on a stalk of hyssop and brazenly rode over to the Lord. Raising it to His lips and mouth, Cassius persuaded Him to quench His thirst. Demons mocked nearby.

Holding it at His face, Cassius, again pressed it forcefully against His lips. Repulsed, the thirsting Jesus rejected it, drinking from His Father's cup instead. Jesus turned His face, leaning back against the cross, hearing the angry guard yell, "If You are the King of Jews, help Yourself!"

Cassius threw the rag tipped spear to the ground, his horse trampling over it. "Father," Jesus called out with all His heart, "forgive them!" He cried. "They know not what they do!" The heart-breaking, guttural plea from Jesus for those who had pierced Him so viciously, echoed, vibrating through to the heavens. A force of Angels formed shoulder to shoulder as Jesus drew near to His final breath. They comforted and strengthened Him, amazed at His love for the people.

Mother approached the foot of the cross as Mary reached up for His feet again. It was noon and a very thick, tangible darkness swiftly blew through, sweeping over the land for three *very long*, very hard and painful hours.

Suddenly, in a loud voice, "Eloi, Eloi, Lèma sabachthani!" *roared through the land* as Jesus cried out to His Father. "My God! My God! Why have You forsaken Me?" He repeated with a loud, guttural cry such as no human had ever made. Jesus anguished at His Father's turned face.

"It is finished," He wept, lowering His head and gave up His spirit. Jesus was dead. He Who made every attempt to reach us, was gone. The only one who loved us enough to ensure we would have a way to heaven, was dead.

Darkness *thickly* enveloped the sun and bolts of lightning flashed their threatening *rage* across the heavens, warning of their quick approach. Instantly splitting the heavens, the thunders roared their angry voice as one, and the rain began to fall. The heavens and the earth grieved for Jesus. No birds sang. The sun refused to shine.

Mary stood horrified yet astonished at the strength of her Lord, knowing now more fully the power of His love, and becoming more intimately acquainted with Him now in His suffering death. Exhausted but not faint, Mary moved toward John. Time stood still as the Lord uttered His final words on this earth. No one moved, it seemed. All stood watching Jesus hang lifeless in horrified disbelief.

Cassius fearfully approached the cross trembling and said, "Surely, this was the Son of God." Fear struck his countenance, then remorse descended at the full realization of Who hung before him dead.

Women who had been looking on from a distance drew near. Women who had followed Him during His ministry came from Galilee, Jerusalem, everywhere. The Canaanite woman, once called a dog, and her daughter came to Jesus that day to mourn His suffering death.

Now it being the day of Preparation, the next day was a special Sabbath. Jewish leaders did not want bodies left on crosses during the Sabbath, so they petitioned Pilate to have the legs of those who hung broken and their bodies quickly removed. Knowing this, the guards broke the legs of the first man they crucified, who had hung to one side of the Lord, then the legs of the other man followed. When they drew near to Jesus to break His legs, Cassius instead took a spear and with great force pierced the side of Jesus releasing a sudden gush, rushing and flowing of blood and water fulfilling the Scripture. "Not one of His bones will be broken, they will look on the One they have pierced."

The hour passed quickly as Joseph of Arimathea and Nicodemus gently and inexpressibly touched and unfastened the body of Jesus from the cross. All shuddered as the first nail, *hard* to pull, was removed from the wrist of the Lord, carefully. Mournful, yet braced by a supernatural strength, the men pulled the other nail gently, yet with *force,* from His wrist.

Mary nearly fainted at the sight of Him, overcome by His bloody torture, but stalwart. The largest of the three nails was removed, but the men struggled to get this one out for it was so large, going all the way through both feet and penetrating the blood-soaked wood beam that held Him. With extreme patience Jesus was ever so carefully lowered from the cross, the cloth straps bound Him tight. Laying Him gently, carefully on the knees of His Mother, she wiped the blood and dirt from His battered face and body. Mary slowly touched His feet, kissing them and flooding them with her tears. Her beautiful Jesus, her loving Lord, was dead. His voice that once soothed her bruised and broken soul, forever silenced. His body disfigured, those who loved Him tenderly touched His unrecognizable face. She quickly and lovingly wiped the body fluids from the wounds along His legs and feet. Mary's heart was broken.

Mary, Mother of our Lord held her Son tightly to her bosom, rocking Him and weeping over Him, mourning deeply, sweetly caressing His bruised and bloody face, kissing Him repeatedly. John leaned over the body of his Lord, seeing His pierced side, and buried his face at the ravaged bosom of Jesus, grief-struck and devastated. No one could comfort him, for the depth of his heartache was so great. Mary alone now stood, leaning her head back with her eyes open toward heaven, tears streaming in stunned disbelief. Women wailed in disbelief and heartache.

Mary succumbed with her head bowed, faint and distraught in her grief, kneeling at the feet of the Lord. Bowing and kissing them repeatedly, her tears again washed over them, now pierced and bloody. Thick darkness loomed and rumblings continued as they mourned and caressed the Lord. Tenderly, Mary moved hair from Jesus's face and mouth, brushing away and smoothing out the painfully brutal blows, touching the place of His beard, now torn off, and crying.

The women who served the Lord approached the grief-stricken Mother and Mary and covered them with their cloaks, praying and weeping. John lay collapsed, his face buried at the heart of Jesus.

Gathering their strength as one, the men gently raised and carried the body of Jesus down the summit of Calvary, to a cave on the side of a mountain. Near the place where they crucified Jesus was a garden, and in the garden a new tomb. No one had ever been laid in it before. Being the Jewish day of Preparation, they chose the close location of this tomb. Jesus was taken there for preparation and burial.

Pausing at a flat stone to prepare His body, the women meticulously sponge-washed His wounds with water, clean and pure. Taking spices, they anointed all His flesh from head to toe missing nothing. The scent of sweet herbs and spices filled the area where they mourned. Mother removed the scarf gifted to her by Claudia and laid it under her Son's head. Then, she and the women who loved Him completed His preparations.

Mary poured the flasks of nard made of myrrh and aloes, nearly one hundred pounds, into all the wounds. The sight of her eyes overwhelmed her at the way Jesus had been savagely beaten and executed. *How could anyone be so evil? Why was there so much hate? What had He done wrong?*

Finishing, they lifted His wrapped and prepared body. Mary, careful of their every move, went a little further toward the cave. Arriving, Mother stepped inside the cave and positioned herself at the front of the cold, dusty slab where the head of her Son would rest. Mary, without hesitation, went to the foot of the slab and both women were silent, as if waiting. Alone in the cave's quiet where He would rest, Mary looked at the worn and devastated face of Mother. Somehow, Mother maintained a look of knowing, as if she knew this day would come, more than she had shared. Her tears flowed with no end.

In one step, the carriers of our Lord's body moved into the cave, gently maneuvering Him, and placed Him quietly on the cold slab of stone. His body, now wrapped in a long white cloth called *hunger*, meaning *touch*, now rested. Mother leaned over her Son's wrapped head and kissed Him tenderly, not wanting to lift her lips.

Mary could not be comforted.

Pilgrims and locals gathered at the temple, ready for the lambs prepared by the priests. Blood for the lentils of every home dripped into their round goblets, and passing them down the line of priests, the *last* priest took the blood, covering the altar. The time of the Passover meal was here.

HIS OWN RESURRECTION

Saturday

It was early in the morning *the next day.* Mary stood alone in a dim-lit room, a soft fire-flame danced quietly, keeping the stones warm for the first breads to bake, soon they would be heated. A soft rain fell steadily, soaking the parched soil. *A dense, solemn* thickness spread across the moonlit sky, clouding its light for moments at a time.

"I love the rain," she whispered, peering through the lattice window at the darkened moon, talking to herself. Her thoughts fell back to her childhood when she first found the *dove-ling. It was so long ago.*

Standing by the fire, Mary stared, dazed and frozen-*still* in time. She replayed each horrific image and sound of the last two days*: the screams of the people; the silence of the Lord.* The hiding disciples had not looked for them, fearful of arrest, or worse. Mary waited for the third day.

Mother, in another room wept in her sleep, *mourning Jesus.* Watchful angels stood all around, covering her. None could see their splendor.

Mary moved quietly through the shared home while many mourners slept, exhausted from their crying. The women who followed Jesus and several young women and children had gathered in Mother's home, finding peaceful comfort with each other's love for Him.

"The Lord is my Shepherd; I shall not want," Mary tearfully moaned in despair, a slight melody emerging from her lips. The sound of mourning rose within her. Warning away the pain of her grief, Mary dried her eyes, again. *"Although I walk through the valley of the shadow of death, I will fear no evil... He's gone,"* she choked back. As if talking to Jesus directly, Mary said, *"I fear no evil, Lord,"* touching the broken alabaster piece held on a strand of leather, hanging just over her heart.

"Your ways are higher," she sang to the Lord, trying to comfort herself. *"Your thoughts are higher; more than anything, I've ever loved in life... You're more than any man I've... ever loved,"* she wept, her heart longing for His presence. *"Your ways are higher..."* she cried, singing.

Her soul replayed the **fresh horrors** of His image, helpless and silenced. Mary leaned over the table to lay her bowls and spices, not able to contain her grief. Seized with emotion, choking back her despair, images of the cross and His suffering filled her mind and Mary *fell to the floor* wrapped in her garment, undone. The force of evil all around her wove lies of deception as she mourned. The voice of death *swirled* all around her, wickedly hissing, *"Your Savior is a dead liar."* Echoing through her, deception rang loud, taunting, *"All is a lie, a trick!"* The tongue of Lucifer slithered, desperately, *"Who is there to raise Him? Jesus is dead."*

"Jesus?" she called, rising from the floor as if He were standing beside her. Seeing the mourners stir, Mary settled herself at the table, facing the broken alabaster flask. Before she could make another sound,

she lay her head down, weeping. "All the wonderful things He taught me," she cried. "Jesus?" she called out as she fell sleep.

"It will be daybreak soon," came a gentle voice from behind. *"Come* Mary, it's almost time." Joanna smiled, softly shaking her to wake. Startled, Mary turned to see Joanna and her tears rushed forth as she mustered a smile, embracing her friend. *"I feel Him with me, even now sister,"* Mary confessed bursting into tears.

"Today, we must care for His body," Joanna whispered, helping Mary gather herself, wiping her tears. "The Lord would want to know what *all your tears* are about, Mary," she laughed, holding back her *own* grief and heart-struck sorrow. The women knew what they needed to do. Waking the others, Joanna returned to the table to collect their vessels, ointments, and wraps.

Leaning on the chair to support herself, Mary rose to her feet, wobbling the table, nearly tipping the broken *flask* of oil. As she hurried to catch it, her thoughts took her to the moment she anointed Him *only days ago* at the home of the Pharisee, the *father of a betrayer.* Her memories were so fresh, sensing the power of the moment she anointed the Lord's head and feet that night. She bundled the last of the myrrh, packing it carefully, and *lit her torch* for their journey to the tomb.

With briskness in their steps and a heavy song on their heart, the women made their way to the tomb. In the thick of *darkness and quiet* they rushed to continue the traditions for burial, in ministering to the body of Jesus, while everyone slept and disciples hid.

In another dimension, *occurring simultaneously,* a violent assault was taking place at the gates of hell. Jesus prevailed against the enemies' gates and an *angelic host of warrior's tread* down the adversary of God's people.

The power of the Resurrection of Jesus blasted through every heavenly sphere as the Lord of All rose from the dead and re-entered our world. The graves of many opened at the tearing of the veil when Jesus was crucified, and now the *resurrected bodies* of the saints who *had* died, rose. Coming out of the graves after His Resurrection, they made their way into the holy city, appearing [6] to many. *Jesus was resurrected!*

EARLY SUNDAY MORNING

Turning up the hill, *the brightness of the torches before them,* the women paced themselves well, arriving jubilant. Soon they would minister in this most *respectful way* to His deceased body, as they loved Him so much.

"Who will roll away the stone for us?" asked Mary, feeling much better than earlier. "It's so very *huge!"* Winding up the path her eyes searched turning to find the tomb when she sharply halted, dropping her bowls, blindly reaching for the women. Guards on the ground in stunned bewilderment tried to regain their bearings. Cassius sat facing the tomb. Seeing and realizing the danger he faced, he raced to his horse and rode to inform Pilate while others scrambled, racing behind him in a panic.

"What has happened?" Salome screamed startled and taking a step back, *"The stone!"*

"Who has done this? *Someone* has... *How?"* Oblivious to anyone else, Mary stood *stunned* and bewildered at what she saw. "Where is Jesus?" she whispered, beneath her breath.

The massive boulder, *multiple* guards had struggled to roll, was not in its place! The reinforcements that once *secured* the boulder were *burst and scattered.* With surprise and confusion, the alarmed women stared at the tomb's entrance. Turning, they all saw an angel of the Lord *standing in brilliant light* and were in awe, speechless. Arrayed in splendor and perfection, he spoke saying, *"Why do you seek the living among the dead? I know you are looking for Jesus, who was crucified. He is not here! He has come back to life as He promised!"*

---

[6] Matthew 27:52

Looking into the tomb, they saw a young man in a long white robe sitting on the right. So alarmed, the women fell back, bowing and shielding their faces. A second magnificent angel emerged inviting, "Come! *See the place where His body was, then go quickly and tell His disciples He has come back to life! He is going ahead of them into Galilee."*

Fading in brilliance, the angel further instructed her, stating, *There, they will see Him. Note **all** I have told you."*

Trembling and astonished, the women remembered fully, the promise of Jesus to rise from the dead *on the third day!*

"Mary!" screamed Salome, as Mary turned running to find the other disciples. Afraid and confused, *not knowing what to imagine,* but knowing fully what she had *just* seen and heard, Mary ran to find Peter.

Arriving at the home, Mary burst through the doors startling everyone to their feet. Seeing Peter and John, she blurted out in distress, shouting, *"He's gone! They have taken Him! We don't know where they have put Him!"*

Bolting through the door, Peter and John raced ahead of the women who followed as quickly as possible through the winding, rocky path. John outran Peter reaching the tomb *first.* Bending over and looking in, he fixed his gaze on the strips of linen perfectly *folded and placed* on the stone that bound Christ's lifeless body before him, but *dared not* go in. Then Peter came rushing behind him, straight into the cold, dark, dusty tomb.

Seeing the linen strips folded and placed neatly to the side, *as well as* the cloth that wrapped around Jesus's head, *Peter grabbed his own head* in disbelief, falling to his knees. *Overwhelmed* with dismay at the sight of the Lord's missing body, his mind raced with confusion, his face wrought with despair, not knowing what to think. Jesus was gone!

The cloth lay in its place, separate from the linen, radiating the glory of God. The presence of Holiness filled the space of the cave. John, who had reached the tomb first, finally went all the way in, shaken with astonishment.

The men questioned among themselves, perplexed, as the women drew near the mouth of the caved tomb, peering in. Catching up with them from the path, Mary wept in disbelief, nearing the stony entrance. Peter, *about to leave*, approached her, pausing *as if to speak*. Lowering his head, instead, he returned to the path without a word, making his way back to the place where they were staying. Almost immediately John followed briskly, catching up with him as they rushed back to tell the others.

THE APEARANCES

The women collected themselves and together proceeded to approach the empty tomb, holding each other close, leaning on the cave's stony entrance. Gazing at the rolled away stone and its massive size, they soon realized no human alone could have moved it. Struck with awe and trembling, they leaned further into the opening of the tomb, making room for each other and for Mary, who was drawing slowly closer, that they may peer cautiously at the glory of the Lord and what remained.

One by one the women returned to the footpath, mourning. They believed someone had robbed the tomb of Jesus's body, in the night. Refusing to leave and abandon her duties, the distressed Mary remained at the entrance of the cave, crying softly, unsure of what to do next. Stepping into the tomb alone, she saw two angels in white seated where Jesus's body had been. One at the head, the other at the foot, they looked at her when one asked the reason for her great, sorrowful anguish. "Woman," he called, gently, "why are you crying?" Collecting herself she responded, in a daze, "I don't know where they have taken my Lord." Mary turned to follow the women as they disappeared around the bend, when she caught a glimpse of a man tending graves. Clearing away brush and debris, she heard a voice call her way, "Woman! Who are you looking for?"

"They have taken my Lord away and I don't know where they have put Him," she cried with all her heart. Turning, she suddenly saw Jesus standing there but still did not realize it was Him. Continuing to think He was the gardener, she pleaded out loud, "Sir, if you have taken Him away tell me where and I will get Him."

"Mary," came the sweet sound of the voice of the Lord. She recognized Him and jumped turning so quick, nearly falling over herself, reaching out for Him. "Rabbi!" she cried, but Jesus would not allow Himself to be touched.

"Do not hold on to Me," He warned. "I have not yet ascended to My Father."

Her quivering fingers reached hard for Him, though painfully refraining to touch Him. Trembling, her eyes spilled over with tears. Mary could hardly compose herself, not able to take her eyes off Him. She quickly realized He was in a glorified state and fell to her knees, amazed and worshipful.

The beauty of His radiant presence lifted her, filling her with wonder and awe, a great fullness which calmed her restless spirit. The cares of the world, and all of Mary's weakness and the tiredness in her body dissipated, as a wondrous light emanated from His entire being. All her fears dissolved all her tears dried up! Jesus was alive!

"Go, instead," He instructed her. "Tell My brothers, I Am ascending to My Father and your Father, to My God and your God." Mary clung hard to His words. The glory of God enveloped the entire area encapsulating the two of them alone, then quickly faded. Only the chirps of birds were heard.

She pressed her hands over her heart trying to catch her breath; her finger touched the broken alabaster piece. Speechless and startled at His appearing, Mary realized what had just happened. She regained her composure, standing to her feet and swiftly headed down the grassy path to the home where the disciples were hiding.

I have seen the Lord! was all she could think of, racing toward the disciples. A flood of emotions filled her soul overtaking her as tears flowed over her entire face. Flooding her mind, heart, spirit and soul, her song quickly became, "I have seen the Lord!"

"I have seen Him!" she shouted. Unashamed, running through Jerusalem to the upper room where the hiding disciples remained, she knocked, quickly looking around to see if anyone had seen her. Entering and quickly closing the door, she made her way to the kitchen where Joanna helped her with her cloak.

"You look radiant Mary, what has happened?" asked Joanna surprised at her countenance.

"Hush, where is Susanna, and the others?" Mary asked, breathless and hurried.

"Preparing to eat. They're

127

all still so troubled and tired; they hide, still," she added. "I know you are famished." Taking her cloak and laying it over a side-stepstool, Joanna added, "Here... water to wash your feet." Taking a wash bowl from the shelf, Mary placed it on the floor by the stool.

"Tell me, *please*," asked Susanna softly, entering the room.

"I see Him on your face! What is it, Mary?" Sarah asked, seeing a fresh glow about her. There was something different about her eyes.

"He is very much with us, sisters. Let us get to the others and I will share all that I have seen." Rushed, she quickly dipped her feet in the water-bowl, splashing water everywhere, grabbed a towel, dabbed her feet, and rushed for the stairs ahead of them all.

Making their way up, the women lowered their voices as the sound of the disciples became clearer. Their restless fear was all that remained to taunt their imaginations when Mary came crashing through the door. Startled to their feet, they turned to see Mary and the women crowded at the doorway, when Mary declared, "I've seen Him!" The disciples, dumbstruck, snickered but gathered around when she said, again, "Peter, I've seen the Lord! He spoke!"

John, without a hesitating thought, ran to Mary. "He spoke?" he asked, hopeful, his eyes filling with tears.

"Sister," Peter began, "we know He trusted you. What do you mean? Spare no detail."

With a light in her eyes, Mary boldly declared, "I saw Him, alive, Peter! He wouldn't let me touch Him but said, 'Go. Tell My brothers I am ascending to My Father and yours, to My God and your God.' He goes before us to Galilee." Sarah, Joanna, and Susanna crowded just behind her, in prayer, listening to her every word, knowing in their heart it was all true.

Outraged and appalled, Andrew burst forth frustrated, yelling, "Us? Did the Lord speak with <u>you</u> in <u>place of a man</u>? You are His messenger, now? Secretly?" Turning to Peter, Andrew angrily demanded, "Are we to listen to her?"

Distraught by his demeanor, Mary turned pleadingly to him, saying, "I've seen Him! I..." Turning to them all she continued, "Brothers, do you think I imagine this or would lie about Him?"

John, still amazed at the possibility, neared Mary solemnly, and asked, "Is it possible?" The room fell silent.

From the back of the room, Levi stepped forward and facing Mary, spoke saying, "I believe you." Then, turning to Andrew, he continued, "If Jesus made her worthy, who are we to reject her? He trusted her." Approaching Mary, Levi lovingly addressed her, saying, "You have done so much for us all, sister. Our Rabbi held you in high esteem and so should we."

Andrew, not holding back a word, blurted out, "A woman? I will not!"

Peter, rising to her defense, interjected against his brother, loudly, "Enough, Andrew!" Then turning to Mary, he said, "God will use you." The room fell silent, again.

Thomas and the disciples, in near unison and perplexed, asked, "What? How? Not possible!"

But Mary wanted to know more. "What do you mean and how?" Approaching her seriously and in a calm tone, Peter said, "It is absurd God would speak through a woman, yet He does. You."

Now standing face to face with Mary he continued, wholeheartedly, "Jesus trusted you, Mary. You have helped us understand His mysteries. I believe you have seen Him, sister. I believe He will use you, still." Facing the roomful of followers, Peter added, "Jesus accepted her and all these women as equals. So, shall we." With this, the women quietly agreed, glad to hear a fellow brother defend a sister who also loved Jesus.

Without hesitation, John stepped forward, saying with a huge smile, "I'm not afraid. I want to see Him." Turning to them all, he added, "I want to see Jesus." The divided disciples disputed even more, until Thomas left in a hot rage. John though, and Peter, the disciples and women, encouraged Mary, eagerly wanting to hear more.

They hurried to lay utensils for eating, smiling discreetly among themselves. Susanna brought out washing bowls and the disciples washed their hands. Joanna laid loaves of bread at the center, head, and foot of the table, while others brought pitchers of water, meat and herbs. Mary, who had quietly removed herself, washed her hands again on another table, to the side. Approached by Andrew, they soon talked calmly and apologetic, reassuring of his devotion to them all.

The sound of laughter grew as the meal and portions passed around the table. The conversation continued to ease among the friends, as they tried to adjust without Jesus, strengthening each other with each passing hour. They spoke of their love for the Lord and what He meant to them, and their faith was reinforced by the stories they shared.

ROAD TO EMMAUS

That afternoon while on the road to Emmaus, Cleopas, the brother of Mother's deceased husband, and his companion, struggled with Mary's story. They considered the reports of the empty tomb and Mary seeing and speaking to Jesus, with doubts, when as if out of thin air, Jesus appeared jumping in on their conversation.

"What are you discussing?" He asked the troubled travelers. "The Resurrection," Cleopas answered. "We come from the place where it happened," he continued, not recognizing the Lord.

"Have you heard?" his companion asked. "Do you believe?" Jesus had veiled their eyes as He had Mary's when she thought Him to be a gardener.

"How foolish you are and slow to believe all that was foretold by the Prophets," responded Jesus. "Did not the Christ have to suffer these things first and then enter His glory?" And with that Jesus began to teach them of Moses and the Prophets explaining what was shown through the Scriptures concerning Him, teaching them what was hidden in the Old Testament and what it revealed about Him.

Later, while eating with them, Jesus took bread and broke it, giving it to them by *putting it in their mouths*. It was *then* that the eyes of their understanding opened, and they knew it was Jesus. Immediately the Lord disappeared as they looked upon Him in sheer amazement. With great joy they rushed back to Jerusalem to share all that they had experienced and witnessed of the Lord, saying, "It is true! He is alive!"

Mary greeted them at the door, glad to hear them testify to the amazement of the others. Mother stood calmly, knowing the Scriptures were being fulfilled. With the disciples scattered throughout the room and the doors locked, all were intently listening to every detail the two witnesses reported, when suddenly Jesus appeared before them, walking effortlessly through the wall. Before they could react, He was standing in the room.

"Peace to you all!" He calmly greeted them, smiling with great gladness. Terrified to the core, the women all screamed, drawing back, falling over each other, but Mary fell to her knees. Mother, amazed at the glory radiating through her Son, smiled, noticing the fragrance in the room had suddenly changed. Angels flanked the room, standing all along the walls, though only Jesus could see them. They honored Him in their stand.

"Why are you afraid?" He asked approaching His friends, staring back in awe. "Why do you have doubts? Look at My hands and feet and see that it is really Me," He urged. "Touch Me and see for yourselves! Ghosts don't have flesh and bones, but you can see that I do." Showing them His hands and feet, He allowed them to touch Him.

Mary reached out for Jesus first. He smiled upon her and blessed them all, saying, "God's peace to you! As My Father sent Me, I send you," laying hands on each of them, deliberately. Blowing on them gently, He whispered, "Receive the Holy Spirit. If you forgive sins, they are forgiven. If you retain the sins of any, they are retained. I'm hungry now!" He smiled, taking a seat, and was quickly served broiled fish and honeycomb with hot bread, olives, and raisin cakes with figs.

Eating with them He furthered His teaching so they could more fully understand, saying, "These are the words I spoke to you while I was still with you. I told you everything written about Me in Moses's Teachings, the Prophets and Psalms *had* to come true." He reminded them, commanded them all to continue His work, exhorting them, "The Scripture said the Messiah would suffer and that He would come back to life on the third day. The Scripture also revealed that by His authority the people would be told to turn to God and change the way they think, act and live. This way, <u>sins are forgiven</u>. This would be told to people from all nations, beginning in Jerusalem. You are witnesses to these things. Friends do not leave Jerusalem, but wait for the gift My Father promised, which you have heard Me speak about. For John baptized with water but in a few days, God will baptize you all with the Holy Spirit. You will receive power when the Holy Spirit comes upon you and you will be My witnesses, telling people about Me everywhere, in Jerusalem, Judea, Samaria and to the ends of the earth."

As quickly as He appeared, Jesus was gone. Silence fell over the roomful of people, and Mary wept with joy.

FIRST NIGHT
John 20: 19-24

The disciples, crestfallen and confused, fearfully hiding, repeated the events of the last several hours. Reassuring themselves of the miracle, Andrew beamed, saying, "It is *true!* Just as Jesus said it would happen, it has I believe you, sister. He showed Himself to you!"

But late into the evening, Thomas, who had stayed away from the rest even after being told they had also seen Jesus, continued with foolish determination to debate, and argued to the dismay of them all, repeatedly. Shaking his head, unashamedly, after stirring up much contention, Thomas stated, defiantly, "Unless I see, unless I touch His side, I will not believe!"

Hurt, and anguished by his incessant doubt, Mary bolted for Thomas, "Is it not enough, Thomas, what He has suffered? Repent of your cruel doubt," she screamed, reaching for him, for what had further broken her heart: his doubt.

Andrew and James quickly blocked her, turning her to the women who rushed, hushing her. John approached her to help. "Your doubt makes you weak!" she screamed over them. Peter stepped abruptly toward Mary, as if to restrain her, but Martha stood, blocking him, then the women also, warning him away with a look. Peter paused and returned to the men. "See?" shouted Thomas, "She's not changed! A rude emotional woman! Look at her!" Peter's eyes set on Thomas, silencing him with one glance.

Thomas's outrageous remarks of doubt and unbelief at the Resurrection of Jesus, struck Mary with heartfelt indignation and a rush of emotions overtook her. He had seen so much, to be filled with doubt as he was. Other disciples intervened, assuring Thomas, and trying to convince him, who drowned himself in doubt. He refused to acknowledge the possible miracle.

EIGHT DAYS LATER–Thomas

John 20:6-29

A week later the disciples were in the house again. Thomas remained close since the outburst. The doors were locked, yet without a sound and without warning Jesus entered, walking through the wall! All were startled, screaming and falling back over themselves when Jesus passed through calmly, saying, "Peace! Peace be with you all!"

Then turning to Thomas specifically, Jesus directed him, "Put your finger here," He said pointing to the wounded side, pierced by the spear, near His heart. "Reach out your hand and put it into My side, brother," Jesus instructed, walking toward him. "See My hands," stretching them toward the trembling, doubtful disciple. "Stop doubting, Thomas, and believe! Settle your faith!" Jesus stressed as Thomas crumbled, falling hard on his knees.

With cautious, yet hopeful hesitation, shocked at the sudden appearance of the Lord, Thomas gently moved toward His wounded side. A tear ran down his doubt-riddled face. All in the room stood motionless, struck by the splendor of Jesus and His appearing. Thomas's thoughts quickly replayed a slow reel of the many moments where the miraculous had occurred and he had witnessed the glory of God, for himself.

"Thomas!" called out John. "He changed water into wine before our very eyes."

"And fed thousands with bread and fish," called Andrew. "Brother," whispered Peter. "He walked on water to us, and Lazarus! Is anything *too hard* for Him?"

Thomas, weeping now, stretched his trembling hand nearer, toward the piercing of His side. I said, 'Let us go, that we may die with Him,' boasting, like a fool," Thomas remembered, aloud. "I saw You captured and flogged, led like a lamb to the slaughter, silent," looking to Jesus. "I saw You carry Your own cross up Golgotha's hill, staggering,

134

falling and beat... bleeding, only to get up *again and again and again,* to finish Your race; then crucified, he cried, "now, You stand before me, alive? *How?*"the doubtful, distraught disciple wept out loud.

His fingers reached for the horrific *open wound* near His breast slowly, most tenderly gliding them the full length past his wrist, as the flesh torn wound *swallowed-up* Thomas' trembling hand. Overcome with grief and shame at his cowardice, Thomas fell face down to the feet of Jesus, wrapping his face in the hem of His garment. Agonized, he wailed out a cry from the core of his being, "My Lord and my God! *Jesus!*"and fell flat on his face, repenting and full of regret.

"Because you have *seen* Me, you have believed," Jesus whispered, "but *more blessed* are those who have *not seen* and yet have believed."

Thomas wept uncontrollably and overrun with anguish of soul. The remorse struck man, surrounded by his fellow disciples, grieved, in deep devastation, inconsolable.

Thomas wept, mourning himself to sleep.

HIS ASCENSION & THE BAPTISM OF FIRE

Making their way through the village toward the home where the Twelve remained, Mary continued to encourage the women. More continued to come, joining them, strengthening their purpose to spread the news of the Resurrection. At the start of a bustling morning, both Mary's prepared to meet with the disciples, whom they had not seen in days.

"Mary don't forget to bring salts," called Mother, "I'm sure they need a good foot-washing by now!" laughing with renewed strength.

Mary reached for the salts, replying, "Yes, I am sure," she laughed. "This journey has been longer than life itself. I'm sure they continue in derision, Mother," she speculated. No one had seen the men since Mary lunged at Thomas.

Upon arriving, they entered testifying of all they had heard: *the graves of many dead opened the day of the Lord's Resurrection.* Many others from throughout Jerusalem reported they received their *loved ones* back from the dead, to the shock of everyone in the region.

Although, excited to hear, several of the disciples were still grievous and heavy-laden.

THE CATCH OF FISH
John 21:1-14

Peter, Thomas, Nathanael, John, James, along with Andrew and Levi huddled together, growing more despondent. The days without Jesus had no end, for them. Remembering the water, and how Jesus loved being in the boat over it, Peter had gone to the shore followed by his friends. Looking out over the sea, he called out to them, "I'm going out to fish."

The heavy-hearted disciples replied, "We'll go with you!" gathering their things and departing early. After a long night, they caught nothing.

It was early the next morning, when drawing near to the shore, a voice carried by the wind came to them, "Friends, have you caught any fish?" It was Jesus calling out.

"No!" they answered in frustration, not bothering to see Who it was. "Throw your net on the *right* side of the boat; you will find a lot!" Hesitant, the disciples looked to Peter, unsure of what to do.

The leader raised his voice, "We've fished *all night* catching nothing. It's morning now and You say, *cast to the other side?*" Concealing his frustration, he failed to hide his sarcasm. Motioning abruptly for the men to cast the net, it had hardly hit the water when within moments, it was so full they could not lift it. Unable to haul it in because of the large, heavy catch, John and Peter turned, recognizing the Man who stood by the fire.

"Lord!" yelled John with his whole heart, ecstatic when he realized Who stood before them waving. As soon as Peter heard, *Lord!* He wrapped himself in his outer garment, jumping straight into the water. He plunged headfirst into the water, pushing his body through the

137

currents, forcing back the waves. Pulling himself through the water's resistant force, all he could see was the face of Jesus. He feared not the waves as before but fixed his gaze on Him Who waited on the shore. Peter's thoughts recalled how much he missed Jesus, how much he wanted to touch Him and hold Him. He swam the distance, not considering the challenge of the current, nor his own sinking, as when the Lord pulled him up and out of the waves. Peter swam to Jesus, without a single thought to himself.

The stunned disciples followed in the boat, towing the net full of fish as they were still about a hundred yards from shore. Landing, they saw a beautiful fire of burning coals with fish and bread heating over it. "Come ashore!" the Lord called out. "Peter!" Jesus hollered, "Bring some of the fish you just caught!" Peter climbed back into the boat dragging the net ashore full of exceptionally large fish, 153 in all, but even with so many, the net did not tear. "Come," Jesus called out loud to them all, "have breakfast with Me." He smiled, pulling whole, fat fish from the open fire.

Over the next several weeks the Lord appeared to the believers, repeatedly in Galilee and Judea. They worshipped Him wholeheartedly and He blessed them, exhorting continually, "All authority in heaven and on earth has been given to Me, and I pass it on to you all. So, make disciples of all nations and people everywhere you go. Baptize them in the Name of the Father and of the Son and of the Holy Spirit, as you have seen and heard Me do. Teach them to obey everything I have taught you and even commanded you. Remember, I am always with you, to the end of the age."

Hundreds, *Mary, and her family among them,* witnessed the appearing of the Lord after He rose and prior to His Ascension, forever changing them.

THE ASCENSION OF JESUS

Acts 1:6-26

Finally, as the disciples of men and women walked along the path on a route from the Mount of Olives, the Lord was suddenly with them, again. Joining the conversation, He greeted them with great joy! He led them out as far as Bethania, after much informative and joyous conversation, sharing their provisions as they walked. Suddenly and without warning, Jesus turned to bless them, but there was something different about it, this time.

Lifting His hands, a misty cloud-like glory enveloped Him while He spoke. Straining to see Him through the cloud, they noticed Him being carried up, lifted high up to heaven, right before their eyes. The witnesses then saw two white-robed men, angels, suddenly standing in front of them. "Men of Galilee," one called out loudly, "why are you staring into heaven? Jesus was taken from you but someday *He will return* in the same way you saw Him go," their magnificent presence disappearing with the misty cloud, as they finished speaking. A thick silence came over the witnessing disciples, who quickly realized further the consistency and progression of these incredible supernatural events.

"No one will believe this," Thomas whispered, finally breaking the silence.

Staring straight into the empty spot where Jesus stood, just moments before, Mary answered back, "Yes, they will." Nodding, slightly, reassured within herself, she repeated to them all, "Yes, they will!"

With so much to absorb, the group solemnly returned to Jerusalem from the Mount of Olives. Arriving, they went straight to the upper chamber of the house where they continued to stay, away from the rest of the world.

OUTPOURING OF THE HOLY SPIRIT
Acts 2:1-47

Devout Jews, from every nation under heaven gathered early in Jerusalem, as they had for generations. The memorable season was still very much upon them and arriving at the *fiftieth day,* since the Passover and Jesus's crucifixion. Their spring, harvest festival was at hand.

The streets were bursting with a huge mix of people, overcrowding the market and all along to the temple. The excitement of vendors trying to sell their items, flawed, and spotted *still,* lured the people to their rickety tables, even if just for shade. It was business as usual in the mechanics of their holy traditions, the Pharisees overlooking with content.

THE UPPER ROOM - JERUSALEM
33 A.D.

Peter and the disciples, many remaining together since the Ascension of the Lord *ten days prior,* joined to discuss the events leading up to this day, and the direction they should all take. Now, with the day of Pentecost fully upon them, the mixed crowd had greatly multiplied. The Twelve, with Judas replaced by Matthias, had managed to gather in one place, in full agreement with each other, *united in prayer and purpose* for the first time in a long time. Joined along with them was Mary, the Mother of Jesus, Salome, Joanna, Susanna, several other women, and the half-brothers of Jesus: James, Joses, Jude, Simon and their sisters closely among them. Mary, Martha and Sarah stayed close to Mother, along with John. When the Seventy finally arrived with Lazarus, Maximin and Sidonius, there were 120 believers in one place. Peter, his heart full, stood to encourage them all.

"Brothers," he began, "the Scriptures **had to be fulfilled** concerning Judas who guided those to arrest our Lord." The disciples solemnly agreed, some shaking their heads, while others bowed theirs.

140

Still drowning in a mix of opinion, wrought with frustration, none wanted to speak for lack of words. The shock of that day's events, *only fifty days prior*, continued to grieve and perplex them all, piercing their hearts sore.

"It's most urgent," Mary stood to exhort, "that we remain close and supportive of each other," encouraging the group. "Fear is rampant throughout with all the confusion and rambling on from leaders who know nothing," she continued, helping to lay the meal portions before them. "We must strengthen our unity as a body of believers. We are witnesses of His glory and the mandate is on us *to tell all that we know to be true.*"

Smaller groups formed discussions as they ate, and she and the women discussed other important details of how to best organize when their conversations took a sudden turn. All in the room sensed the obvious shift in the atmosphere. A thickness filled the room, tangible.

Mary, the *Mother of Jesus*, moved nervously toward John as he reached for her, when a sudden rush of sound approached them with great acceleration. Not knowing where the loud sound was coming from, the frightened 120 clustered toward each other when a thunderous vibration rumbled. A deafening, torch-like flaming sound drew nearer and louder, surrounding them all. Intense awe came over the 120 when they saw they stood in that same *misty cloud-like* thickness that surrounded Jesus when He ascended, only *this* fell from heaven, suddenly. It came directly above them, a sound like a *mighty rushing wind*, filling the entire house where they gathered. What appeared like *divided tongues of fire* was visibly resting over them; the swirling fire seen blazing, burning nothing. And they were all *filled* with the Holy Spirit of God and spoke in other tongues, distinctly clear, and articulate as the Spirit of God gave them utterance.

Now, being filled with power from God's Holy Spirit themselves, they rose one by one, turning to see God's glory on each other's faces. This heavenly language flowed like an unstoppable river, a *broken* dam.

As the powerful sound blasted throughout the city, it shook all and alarmed the multitude. They rushed together, perplexed and questioning among themselves, scattering through the streets. Vendors, bewildered and near panic with the others, heard the 120 speak in his own language praising the Name of the Lord. Uttering the greatness of God, the Apostolic disciples lifted their praise to heaven, amazing everyone. One rose to lead the clamor, saying, "What has happened? These people are drunk!"

A religious leader in the crowd raised his voice over the commotion, "Are not all these who speak, Galileans? How is it they speak our native language?" pointing to the crowd, "Parthians and Medes, Elamites and residents of Mesopotamia," he pointed out bewildered, "Judea, Cappadocia, Pontus and Asia, Egypt and Libya, visitors from Rome, both Jews and proselytes, even Arabians! We hear them in our own tongues, telling the mighty works of God!" he exclaimed in shock.

All were amazed and perplexed, saying to one another, "What does this mean?" Others, to gain an audience, mocked them, saying, "They are filled with new wine," one drunkard called out, "drunk, that's all," and repeatedly gestured his sport of the 120, trying to taunt them who remained unmoved.

Full of God's power and authority, *magnifying the greatness of God,* it was a new day and only God could move them.

PETER PREACHES

Now, the newly baptized 120 further spilled out into the streets praising the Lord in the power of their baptism. A great boldness covered them all like a shield. Mary emerged from behind the new Apostles, standing in amazement at the power of God being demonstrated before her. Her eyes fixed on Peter who stepped forward from the rest to address the confounded crowd, boldly. Lifting his voice, he assuredly declared: *"Men of Judea! and all who dwell in Jerusalem,"* the new preacher, thundered. A thick hush raced through the people, falling over the bewildered multitude, eager for answers. Peter continued, *"Let this be known to you and give ear to my words. For these people are not drunk, as you suppose,"* he confirmed.

Mary pressed to capture every word, stepping away from Mother, when Peter continued, even more, in the power of God's anointing, *"Since it is only the third hour of the day,"* he added. "No, but rather *this was that* which was spoken through the prophet Joel, *"In the last days it shall be, God declares, that I will pour out My Spirit on all flesh and your sons and daughters shall prophesy, and your young men shall see visions, your old men shall dream dreams; even on My male servants and female servants in those days I will pour out My Spirit and they shall prophesy. And I will show wonders in the heavens above and signs on the earth below, blood, fire and vapor of smoke. The sun shall turn to darkness and the moon to blood before the Day of the Lord comes, the great and magnificent Day. And it shall come to pass that everyone who calls upon the Name of the Lord SHALL BE SAVED!"* roared the voice of Peter, now an Apostle.

John moved near Mary, poised and flanked by her warrior brothers. Surrounding Mother, they gazed on Peter seeing the power of God overshadowing him. Mary realized she, too, stood in the visible, manifest power of God. His presence fully enveloped them all.

"Men of Israel!" called Peter, his voice rising over the bewildered crowd, "Hear these words!" he implored, earnestly. "Jesus of Nazareth was a man attested to you by God with mighty works! With wonders and signs that God did through Him in your midst, as you yourselves know. This Jesus delivered up according to the definite plan and foreknowledge of God, **YOU CRUCIFIED AND KILLED** by the hands of lawless men. **God** raised Him up, breaking loose the pangs of death for it was not possible for it to hold Him. For David said concerning Him, '**I saw the Lord** always before me, for He is at my right hand that I may not be shaken; therefore, my heart was glad, and my tongue rejoiced; my flesh also will dwell in hope. For You will not abandon My soul to Hades or let Your Holy One see corruption. You have made known to Me the paths of life; You will make Me full of gladness with Your presence.'"

"Brothers," continued Peter, "I know I may say to you with bold confidence regarding the patriarch David, that he both died and was buried and his tomb is with us to this day! Being, therefore, a prophet and knowing that God had sworn with an oath to David that the Lord would set one of his descendants on his throne, foresaw and spoke about the Resurrection of Jesus Christ, that *He* was not at all abandoned to Hades, nor did *His* flesh see corruption. **This Jesus** God raised up, and of that we all are witnesses.

He was exalted at the right hand of God and received from the Father the promise of the Holy Spirit. God has poured this out, that you are seeing and hearing, for David did not ascend into the heavens, but himself says, 'The Lord said to my Lord, 'Sit at My right hand, until I make Your enemies Your footstool.' Let all the house of Israel, therefore know for certain that God has made Him both Lord and Christ, **this Jesus** Whom you crucified."

The Apostles, arrayed in the glory of God, stood shoulder to shoulder, awed and inspired, as the knowledge of the truth of Christ came over the people, opening their eyes for the first time. The tangible presence of the Holy Spirit hovered over and around them all and angels, warrior angels not seen by any of them, stood flanked surrounding them.

Now, when the people heard this, they were cut to the heart with conviction, their faces set like stone, the color of ash coming over them. One in the crowd lifted his voice, fearfully guilty, shouting to Peter and the rest of the Apostles, "Brothers, what shall we do? We are falling into the hands of an angry God!" This truth seized the crowd with great fear.

So, Peter continued addressing them, saying, "*Repent* and be baptized every one of you in the Name of Jesus Christ for the forgiveness of your sins, and you will receive the full gift of His Holy Spirit. For the promise is *for you and for your children* and for all who are far from God; everyone whom the Lord our God is calling to Himself."

Mary's face, radiant with God's peace, smiled, then turning to John and Mother embraced them both.

Joanna stood near Sarah placing her hand gently on her shoulder. With tears in her eyes, Joanna whispered, dryly "I cannot stop weeping, Sarah. Something new and great has just happened."

"Yes! Joanna!" wept Sarah. "This is the glory of God! God is with us now more than ever!"

"Nothing can stop the power of our God," wept Levi, gripped in absolute amazement at the sweeping power of the Holy Spirit. "Everything Jesus said He would do, He has done; we have received power from the Father! Power from Heaven is on us!" cried the overcome Apostle, now baptized in the Holy Spirit and unhindered in his praise.

And with many other words Peter continued to persuade and bear witness, exhorting them all loudly, saying, *"Save yourselves from this twisted generation!"* in the power of God's Spirit. That day, *the first day,* three thousand souls were added to the number of believers.

BIRTH OF A CHURCH

The people devoted themselves to the Apostles' teachings, fellowship, to the breaking of bread and to prayers. A great awe came over every soul. Multiple wonders and signs manifested through them all, now filled with His Spirit. There were no needy among them, for as many as were owners of lands or houses sold them and brought the proceeds to the Apostles to be distributed to all as they needed; Mary leading the way.

"The people are many, they continue to come!" Mary called to the other women. "We have a great responsibility and have been shown by the Lord how to meet the needs." Excitedly, Martha, gathering her possessions, responded, "Yes, sister! We know what to do! Have we not been taught *well enough* by the Lord, Himself? What more could He have done?"

Continuing in one accord they proceeded to collect and to sell their possessions and belongings, Mary among the first leading by example. Day by day, attending the temple together and breaking bread in their homes, they received their food with gratitude, praising God and having favor with each other. The Lord added to their number, daily, those who were being saved, and the hearts of the people were full and content. With fiery passion, Mary continued to serve and grow in her gift, alongside the other women. She also eagerly learned beside her brothers, the Apostles, who lovingly learned from her, as well. Mary the Magdalene was a preacher!

Preaching the Resurrection of Jesus to anyone who would listen, and some who would not, Mary relentlessly pursued saving a person from evil, deceptive hopelessness that surrounded. Well rewarded for her persistence, she labored alongside the Apostles just as diligently and purposefully as they did. The harvest was plentiful and they worked to ensure it was good.

But, with the anointing came persecution. With opportunity there also came adversity. The newly baptized believers, full of hope and love, became aware of the thickened hate directed at all they did and said. Not long after the Resurrection, the faith of the Apostles was tested, by fire.

THE ANOINTING

The power of God was demonstrated through their lives as the sick and the lame were healed at the very shadow of Peter. The lame walked, jumping and leaping, and the deaf heard clearly for the first time! The blind could suddenly see, and devils were cast out of many being won over to the fellowship of followers and believers in Jesus.

Pieces of clothing and aprons that had touched the newly baptized Apostle, were laid on the crippled and dying, by faith. Igniting the power of the Holy Spirit, manifested miracles, signs and wonders began to happen through the hands of the Apostles. With John and Peter leading the way of authority in Christ by simple faith demonstrated, the man at Solomon's Porch, leaped for joy at the healing power of Jesus's Name. The two men of God, anointed by the Holy Ghost, continued in God's power, Mary and the women beside them. The faith of the Apostles, ablaze with demonstrations and miraculous signs following, endured much persecution and hate.

As fierce and horribly increasing as the persecutions against them were, nothing could deter the mission of the saints. With their faces *set like flint* before Him, they determined to mow down vicious lies that worked to erase their testimony. Those who had *seen and known* the Lord, after He rose from the dead, were *all marked for death* and hotly pursued.

Never had they known such unity of faith nor experienced such raw power from God, though. Mary was fiercely passionate in her faith, not willing to be counted as less than the believer in Jesus that she was. Her driving passion had become the spreading of the good news of Jesus Christ and all that He taught her, knowing it would draw all men to Him. Now she was also not willing that any would perish. With the boldness of a lion in her heart, Mary pushed onward, moved with compassion for God's people.

MESSAGE FOR AN EMPEROR

Soon her gift and her message brought her before powerful and influential people. Many had heard about the Lord and her mission, including the ailing Caesar. Mary sought to seize the opportunity to address the Emperor of many warring issues, seeking peace for God's people. She rummaged through her clothes for something nice to wear, not seeing Martha enter, who held something discreetly behind her back. Trying to conceal her smile, Martha noticed Mary's countenance.

"I am extremely glad at the way prepared for you, Mary," smiled Martha. "You are surely favored. Is this the invitation?" she said taking the scroll from the table, its wax seal already broken.

"I received one, yes! Come with me?" Mary asked earnestly. Looking hard at the invitation, unrolling it in her hands, Martha smiled, "I recall when invitations were not extended to you, sister," referring to Simon's rejection of her, "it is good to see that has changed for you. What will I wear?"

Finally, finding a few dresses, she turned to glance at her sister. "The glory of God of course; as I," assured Mary.

Martha looked curiously at Mary, asking, "Are you nervous? He is the Emperor, after all." She grinned.

Mary, as sure as she had ever been, stopped what she was doing and turned again directly to Martha saying, "I've seen Jesus face to face, watched Him die and rise from the dead; Tiberius is just a man." Martha laid the invitation back on the table and responded seriously, "A very *sick* man: he's worsened since the Lord's death."

Finding bits and pieces from several garments, Mary was able to put together a dress for the elaborate occasion, "Much more happened after Jesus died," she reminded Martha. "The baptism of life. I must try, Martha. The hate for our people is increasing by the day," Mary resounded the horrible truth. "I'm more eager to get there, I would say. Will you *come* with me?" she nearly begged, turning to her sister.

"For certain sister; to see Caesar's face when Holy Spirit touches him! Consider me by your side," she smiled, moving closer to Mary.

Pulling out the item she was hiding, Martha continued, "This was mothers'; *our* mother." Martha uncovered a beautiful hair piece set with stones. "It is yours now; fitting for your hair more than mine. Wear this!" said Martha, placing it in Mary's hand.

Taking the old, but beautifully polished pin carefully, Mary lovingly looked at it, a faint smile on her face. Closing her eyes, she raised it to her hair.

That evening Martha, surprised by the array of meats and dainty breads from faraway places, waited for Mary near the banquet tables. Seeing other's approach Caesar, and Mary getting closer, Martha prayed. Standing poised and ready to respond to the Emperor's inquiries, Mary intended to fully represent the Lord and His people. Then, Tiberius summoned her.

"Emperor Tiberius, *I am Magdalene*. Mary of the Tower, in Magdala; a servant of Jesus, the Christ."

The Emperor, interested in what he had heard of her, motioned for her to draw nearer. "Speak freely," he echoed loudly. All hushed to hear her every word, and Martha stepped a little closer.

Her eyes not looking away and with hardly a blink, Mary walked toward the throne of Tiberius, "In your own province, Great Emperor," she calmly began, "Jesus the Nazarene, a holy man used of God to show miracles as God's Son among us, was executed by instigation and collaboration of the priests and final decree of Pontius Pilate, your governor."

A heavy silence filled the room. Mary stood, immovable, looking straight at the ruler.

"Continue," permitted Tiberius, now captured by her every word. "Despite their claims, Great Emperor, and despite their decree to execute the Nazarene," Mary added, "my Lord Jesus *lives!*"

The chamber full of royals and elite quickly responded in jest of her very words, murmuring and chuckling among themselves, but the *servants* in the room listened closely. Mary did not flinch.

"Absurd!" yelled Tiberius, his voice echoing through the court. Stepping toward her, he angrily continued, "You would attempt to deceive your Emperor? No one can rise from the dead," looking to the banquet table where Martha stood, "any more than an egg can turn red!" the sick, enraged Caesar pointed to a boiled platterful.

"Oh! But Caesar, He was witnessed for forty-days after His death; eating, talking, laughing!" she urged, "Hundreds of us saw Him ascend into...!"

"Silence!" echoed the angry voice of the Emperor. Guests gasped, falling silent, again. None dared to move.

Flustered, he turned to his throne, feeble and assisted. Mary calmly walked to the banquet table and took an egg from the large silver platterful. Nestling it to her breast, she turned her gaze to Tiberius again, as he tried to take a seat. Halting at the gasps of his guests, the Caesar quickly turned back toward Mary to see what the restlessness was about.

"His was a message of new life, sir," she said gently, bowing her head, "Great Emperor," she whispered, holding out the egg before him, "you deserve a chance at new life!" [7]Before she could finish her sentence the egg began to turn red as she held it extended toward him. To the shock of all present, the words, *"Christ is Risen"* [7]appeared, emerging on the egg, inscribed by her pen-less hand.

---

[7] www.monasteryicons.com/product/story-of-the-first-easter-egg/did-you-know

The Emperor stood straight, and great awe and amazement shown on the eager faces of all who filled the chamber. Tiberius drew slowly closer, stepping down toward Mary who held the red egg toward him; brilliant as if polished, softened in its hue. Her hands held the miracle, *the sign and wonder* that helped convey her message of a *new life* in Jesus.

Humbly, Mary awaited his response, knowing the Lord's presence had manifested. "Truly, He is risen," was heard whispered through the courts, the people chattered in amazement.

A visibly shaken, Tiberius approached her, "Mary of Magdala!" his voice ran through the shushing court of gathered elite, "woman of God... what saith the Lord?" The mighty Emperor reached for his seat to balance his stand, growing pale.

A thick silence fell over the people reverently, eager to hear what the servant had to say to the feeble Caesar. Now humbled and sitting on the edge of his throne, he too waited to hear her words.

Raising her head to face him she gracefully, stealthily moved closer and began, "The slaughter of Galileans occurred at Pilates' command; their blood mingled with the blood of their sacrifices as they worshipped God. They executed the followers of Jesus for their faith in Him. You, *Great Tiberius*, have the power to stop this!"

Taking a moment to consider her words Tiberius retorted sarcastically, "New life? I am dying!"

But Mary pressed him further, saying, "Jesus came to heal and to save great Caesar; believe in your heart," she urged, with concern.

"Enough!" Tiberius cut in with a loud voice, standing, interrupting her. Moving toward her, Tiberius softened his sound, "you almost *persuade* me Mary of Magdala; almost," taking the egg from her hand. "This," he continued with a smirk, lifting it for everyone to see, *"just a trick!"* he scoffed aloud. "If Jesus had wanted to *heal* me,"

151

Tiberius turned to Mary, "He would have while He lived. Jesus is dead!" he coughed, hacking loudly. "Pilate grieves me with disorder," he finally said, collecting himself, "a fleet of Guards return with him as we speak."

Turning to look her eye to eye, the dying Emperor whispered in a raspy voice, "You're *too late* dear Mary," turning to depart.

Pilate, arriving to face a ferocious Emperor, found himself swiftly banished to Gaul, suffering a horrible death.

No one could have known what horrors awaited the people of God.

PERSECUTION OF THE MARTYRS

36-68 A.D.

A pattern of murderous persecution followed the anointing. As the church experienced great growth, it also experienced great tragedy. Through the campaign to erase the memory of Jesus, multitudes fled. When the raids began, many desperate and terrified people escaped to the caves. The disbursement scattered the people of God, *everywhere*.

It began decades earlier when Herod's grandfather ordered the slaughter of innocent ones, trying to kill the young child, Jesus. Like a plague of death, this hatred and intolerance spread quietly until it reached the heart of all who opposed God's people.

In a few short years there arose from among the leaders of this barbaric assault, a militant Roman-Jew named Saul. This Pharisee hated all Christians. The grievous man assured the inhumane torture of many people *killed for believing* in Jesus. Few people persevered, deprived with starvations no one had ever seen. They saw no end in sight.

On the Road to Damascus *(36 A.D.)*, one hot afternoon, Saul rode with his soldiers, eager to shed innocent blood. In hot, blood-thirsty pursuit, he vowed to mutilate, eradicate and put an end to any and all of God's people he encountered. Saul rode in seething, bloody hate. On route, though, and without warning, a flash of light burst out of nowhere, knocking the bloodthirsty man off his *high-horse* of blasphemous pride, when he heard a voice say, "Saul, why do you persecute Me?" Through a series of events, Saul was taken to the *very home* of the believers he sought to murder. These believers in Jesus laid their hands on him, *praying,* filling Saul with the Holy Spirit, restoring his sight. News of his conversion did not sit well with many Christians, nor with the Apostles, namely Peter. Paul, the *new name* for the new man, full of Holy Ghost power, pursued teaching, preaching and evangelizing. Through great miraculous wonders, now showed through his own faith in God, the transformed man would soon work shoulder to shoulder with all the Apostles. Doubtful, fearful hesitations continued, though, among the believers. None could agree the power of God could *or would* deliver such a man, a murderer of God's people. With time, though, Paul worked feverishly to reach the lost; Peter, leading the way, amid their stark differences.

MARY SLEEPS

Now tired, Mary Mother of our Lord realized her soon impending death as she had long waited to reunite with her Son. John had long cared for her, taking her to the many places where Jesus had walked, taught and where He rose. Often visiting the place of His Resurrection, her heart longed for Him even more.

The Apostles came from afar, Maximin and the Seventy as well, with Peter leading them in prayers. Mother called each one to herself, laying her hands on their heads and whispering God's love to them. Tenderly her hands embraced each face, wiping away the tears of those who had become her sons, her guardians. Peter sent for Mary, who could not be consoled. Their former tensions and disagreements only strengthened their bond, in the love and peace of their Savior. Peter grew protective of his sister in Christ. Gently, he led the distraught but grateful Mary to Mother's side.

Laying her head on Mother's breast, Mary held to the *only mother* she had ever truly known. Mother taught Mary the things that made for legacy, life and love. Soon, the sweet eyes that beheld the King of Glory throughout every stage of life, death and life again would close. Mother longed to behold the beauty of her Son, her Lord *and* her Savior. Mary, the virgin mother of our Lord, was gone.

With Mothers' death, John departed for Ephesus. He joined others in spreading the Gospel when he learned his brother James was jailed and murdered for his faith. The horrific, assaults were severe and swift, relentless as enemies pursued to silence the story of Jesus. At the hands of ruthless blood-thirsty agents, countless were mutilated. Every attempt to *de-humanize* the believers of Jesus Christ, in the vilest and most humiliating way, *was sport* to those who hated God. Devilish were those who killed people for their faith and love of Jesus.

Entrusting Mary to the care of Maximin was among the most loving acts Peter displayed as he neared his departure for Rome. Maximin covered Mary as Peter grew to after the great outpouring on Pentecost, when the first church was born. Soon, the Roman Empire would ban all Jews.

Stephen, a disciple of the Lord and one of the Seventy, stirred the Sanhedrin to a rage. Outside the temple, at the brink of a riot and not long after Jesus' death, Stephen rose against the hypocrites.

Incited by the ruling Sanhedrin, the mob or haters grabbed Stephen, dragging him to the pit. As he prayed for God's mercy, he would suffer death by stoning. It was only the beginning.

THE PURGE

The Apostles, many of the Seventy along with their loved ones, faithful in Christ, were gathered. Collected from prisons, caves, dwellings they were brought to the shores of the Great Sea. Many made desperate moves to escape the massacre. The beautiful Sea, once peacefully inviting, a traditional place for calm meditations, where boats would launch and fishermen brought home their catch, became a place of great sorrow.

Women screamed, beaten worse near the steps of the temple. Throughout the market square they fought back for their right to live and worship. Fighting to protect what was left of their faith, men and women rose to push back the ruthless, pervading evil that sought to destroy *by mass slaughter*, Gods' people. Age mattered not. There was no mercy.

Mary, Sarah and Maximin rushed frantically through the market over dead bodies and wailing survivors. Jews fought off Romans with great courage; many lay slain or were quickly arrested. The panicked disciples ran, hiding with Salome, Sidonius, villagers and field-hands fleeing the terrifying murder of their people. Children ran in shock, separated from parents, confused, not knowing they should hide, or where.

Making their way to the hiding place of fellow believers, the three entered the home, slamming the door wide open, startling everyone to their feet. "Tiberius is dead!" shouted Mary, sweaty and breathless.

"It is madness! Jews flee for their lives!" she cried. "Gathered! Arrested! Killed! They are slaughtering our people!" Mary screamed. Maximin, overcome, cried out, "It is pure lawlessness," he wept. Falling to his knees, he clutched his head, "we must get out of Jerusalem, tonight!" not knowing what to do.

Salome approached Mary, "We risk the same Mary; we have not heard a word from Lazarus or Martha. We fear their arrest." Shocked, Mary travailed, "Everyone is scattered! We have lost Joanna and Susanna!"

"This evil seeks to silence us all!" claimed Maximin. "We are the only witnesses left of Jesus being raised from death! They will kill us!"

With no warning and great force, the door to the home was kicked in as Guards rushed in striking everyone, grabbing Sarah. "Yield

Jews, by order of the new Caesar!" demanded the violent Romans. None could resist their force as they struck hard against the field-hands overtaking them, and Salome was grabbed by force. They struck Mary.

Falling face down, her hair grabbed by a guard, he yanked her up off her feet. The guard tightened his grip, pulling her head back against his chest. Mary screamed, recognizing him. Then she saw Maximin fall, a sword held to his throat.

"Ignore me now, Mary," whispered the gruff familiar guard, his hot breath on her neck. Licking her cheek, "I hear you appealed to Tiberius," smelling her hair. "Stupid woman!" jerking her back, "you'll learn," smirked the violent man, "get out!" pushing her into the night.

Everyone in the home was shackled then dragged to the overflowing, rotting prison.

Suffering saints begged, moaning as rats ate the corpses of the dead. Lazarus and Martha lay huddled, praying and beaten. All were shackled and bleeding. Guards threw screaming, wounded Jews into the overcrowded prison, over each other and on dead bodies.

Mary emerged bruised and covered in blood, breathless and sweaty. Her cut wrist shackled and her dress torn and ragged, she stood near the body of a man. The guard who took her, lay wounded at her feet. Mary dropped the sword grabbing a large rock and rushed to Lazarus, hitting his shackle and breaking it quick. "Help me!" she said looking at his shocked face.

"What did that man *do to you?*" asked a weepy-eyed Martha, her face swollen and scratched. She also stared shocked at Mary's appearance. Looking straight at her sister, a worn but determined Mary replied, "What do they always do?" With one slam of the rock, Mary broke the shackle off her sisters' foot. "He's nearly dead for it," she said, looking at Martha's pale, drawn face and tossing the stone.

Lazarus freed Maximin, Sidonius and others, leading them out of the prison. Mary grabbed the sword and rushed with Sarah and the women.

Running toward the fiery shore, the surviving believers raced to the water, panning for a boat. Some were sunk, some were on fire, others were overcrowded with screaming, fleeing people. So many bodies lay strewn across the bloody sand as they *ran into the water*. Mary recognized many faces, now dead, floating all around her. The old women from the hills, prostitutes, children, riffraff, thugs and rabble. Martha and Salome struggled through the horror, pushing back the bodies.

The back of a young boy's head scanned the madness along the shore. "Mary!" screamed the familiar voice, with all his heart, "Mary!"

In waist deep water, Mary turned to the sound of Josiah calling from the shore. Alone, bleeding, waving and running toward her, he called her name again aloud, full of fear. "Come! Hurry, Josiah! Come on!" she called in a shrill of urgency, trying to reach him. Running toward her, a sword suddenly thrust the boy from behind. "Josiah! *Josi...* No!" screaming in horror, Mary nearly fell to her knees. Pierced through from the back to his chest, his hands extended to the screaming Mary, Josiah looked straight through her, reaching for her, still. "Mary," he whispered, falling to his knees. A Guard stepped on his dying body, moving to pull the sword.

Falling on the wet sand, Josiah, his eyes struggling for life, was barely breathing. Tears fell from the boys' dirt-streaked face. The heartless Guard yanked the sword with ruthless force, extracting a final breath from the boy whose fish and loaves fed the multitude. Mary screamed in horror. Sarah grabbed her turning her to run when Mary *heard Martha scream.*

Lazarus struggled with his shackled ankle through knee-deep water to a small boat, grabbing it. "Over here! Maximin, help me!" cried Lazarus over the horrified crowd. Maximin hurried through to help. Sidonius arrived to help the men flip the boat. It was so heavy.

Sarah and Salome were being pulled with the tide, struggled to balance. Frantic, they boarded with Sidonius' help. Mary tried to reach her terrified sister, who fought to stay above the angry waters.

Her bruised wrist shackled and her scratched face, bloody and bruised, Mary screamed, "Lazarus! Help me! Martha is drowning!" running toward her sister. Martha could hardly stand when her terrified screams shrieked aloud, *"Help me!"* The waves swallowed her gurgling panic. Reaching Martha before the waves could pull her under, Mary waded through bodies of the lifeless when her own feet lost their footing.

"Lazar--!" she tried in vain to scream, just as her head went under.

Lazarus found and grabbed Mary's hair under the forceful waves, pulling her up. Choking, she grabbed his face and beard, screaming, "Jesus!" Seeing Lazarus, she hugged him tightly, and turned, boarding the boat.

Lazarus and Sidonius lifted and pushed Martha into the boat over the distraught women who huddled together soaked, cold and shivering. Seeing the broken shackle on Martha's foot, Salome reached to help stop the bleeding. The men hurried to board as their feet lost their *firm* stand to sinking sand, beneath the raging waves.

Without warning Roman guards pushed boats into the bloody, windswept waters snatching oars from the desperately pleading. With not even a dry piece of bread to sustain them, the screams of the terrified availed no mercy. With fiery destruction raging, they floated into the Great Sea, that *Great Sea* of Galilee.

Terrified, they clung to each other; Martha and Salome sobbing in disbelief. "Hurry! *Harder!* Row *harder!* Sarah!" yelled Mary over the deafening, terrified screams of the people. The frightened survivors rowed *hard,* as fast as they could. The shore faded.

Soul-piercing *screams* of the dying *rose* to the heavens, the slaughter in the distance roared as black smoke rose to a blue sky. The entire shore of the Galilee was ablaze. Over forty thousand slain. Many sold, *many scattered.* Many were children.

Aimlessly tossed by the waves, *enraged at the horrors of hate and injustice,* the martyred slain float. The waters that once carried Jesus to a sinking Peter, stretched bloody as far as the *eye could see.*

Adrift, the oar-less boat, loaded over with exhausted, sleeping survivors floated. Mary and Maximin, awake from the shock, searched every direction; there was no land in sight.

Facing each other, the two could hear only the waves while they watched a burnt-red sunset swallowed by the night.

Banking near the shore, the worn group helped each other disembark. Half-dried, thin and parched, they faced the new land. "How *long* had they been sailing?" Martha asked, falling to her knees. With her worn face toward the wet sand, her fingers dug into the grit. Mary looked ahead, taking a deep breath, "Where are we?" she whispered to herself. Guided by the Spirit of the Lord, they had arrived near Gaul; *Massilia.*

"Thank you, Lord," whispered Martha, hoarsely. A strained Maximin scanned the desolate shore, saying, "Jesus said, *'go into all the world'...* we are surely in the world *now!"* he pointed out, overwhelmed. "But we are not *of the world,"* reminded Mary quickly, "so we *go!"*

Martha sat on the sand looking ahead to the tree line, calling out, "and 'lay hands on the sick' He also said." Sidonius reached to help her up. "And cast out the devils!" chimed Salome. "So, we go; *preach* all we know!" proclaimed Mary loudly. "We *preach?"* Martha blurted turning her whole body toward Mary. "Yes!" said Lazarus, "and raise the *dead!"*

Approaching Mary from behind, Sarah strained to see further inland, asking, "Where *are* we, Mary? Is that *movement?"* Peering ahead, trying to see past the shadowy trees, Sarah's damp skin bristled with fear.

Pointing toward the tree line, she tried to make out what moved in the distance. One by one her eyes focused: natives emerged, then more. In a moment, the entire tree line revealed hundreds of men and boys holding weapons of war, their painted faces intimidating and fearful. Not willing to move an inch, Sarah held her breath. "*Far* from home," warned Mary.

NEAR 48 A.D.

In a boat with few to no provisions, they had escaped the fierce persecution of believers in Christ. Martha, Lazarus, Maximin and Sidonius, Salome, others and a *servant-girl* shielded by the Spirit of the Lord were delivered to the shores of France through the fierce-tempest, unharmed.

The unfamiliar land became home to the famished few as God's Spirit fueled them. Mary, along with the survivors, denounced the false gods of Jupiter, Juno, Diana, Apollo and others. The new evangelists preached Christ's Resurrection boldly near the altars of the pagan gods, leading many villagers to believe in Jesus.

"On the day Jesus rose from the dead He appeared to us *daily,* eating, teaching, *laughing!*" Mary exhorted, sharing all that she experienced. Amazing at her words, the villagers drew near on their own.

"Many others who were dead rose to life!" added Lazarus, "I was dead; now I live!" he exclaimed, to the shock of all gathered. "Our leader," asked one villager, "his son is near death. Does your Jesus heal now?"

Glad to share their faith in His ability, they all followed the skeptical villagers toward their leader and his dying son. "Our leader is king!" hailed one villager, running ahead of the rest.

161

"King?" asked Mary, "I only know of One." Arriving, Mary realized the regions leader was indeed king, and was led to the chamber of a dying boy.

A bed draped with sheers masked a sleeping child. A royal woman wept at his bedside, wiping the child's brow, repeatedly. He was pale and motionless; the smell and *weight* of death overpowered the room. Looking up to see Mary at the doorway the woman called out in a broken voice whispering, "Tonight, my son will sleep with the gods," standing frail. "Come," reaching out her hand to Mary, "see my son."

Mary realized it was the queen, and stepped toward the sleeping boy, "Don't be afraid," she reassured. Drawing near, Mary continued, "only trust in the God of life; there is only *one* God," touching the boys' clammy forehead.

Mary took the queens' hand in hers, "I don't believe I know of your God," replied the weeping queen, overtaken by her grief.

Turning to face the boy, Mary whispered, "He knows you. We must agree in faith, believing," bowing her head. "Father," Mary prayed. The queen looked on with surprise, lowering her eyes, "we pray in the Name of Jesus our Lord," she continued. Humbly closing her eyes, the queen heard, "*Thank you* for life, Jesus. We *choose* life; have mercy, Lord," Mary prayed earnestly fervent, with no change. Then, without warning and to the utter shock of his mother, the boy moaned, moving. The queen gasped, dropping Mary's hand, throwing her body over her dying son, her breath escaping her.

Mary leaned in, seizing the opportunity to speak the Name of Jesus *into* the boy's waking faith, "In your Name, Jesus!" she whispered, in his cold ear. Fluttering softly for a moment, the boy opened his eyes as his mother fell faint, the Name of Jesus on her lips.

Word *roared* through the village-towns and region about the healing miracle of Jesus at the hands of a woman, a *foreigner* to their land. The king's son had been raised from a bed of suffering and death.

THE KING'S COURT

Filled with knights and villagers, Lazarus and the family of followers stood in the king's court, echoing with excitement. Soon, the shush from officials and counselors to the king, made their way through the crowd.

The boy, full of life and vigor, stood with his mother, the queen. The king held his scepter over a bowed head; it was Mary's head. A beautiful corded braid laid across the length of her back. "Mary of Magdala," echoed the king's voice, "You are endued with God's holy presence. Blessed are you in this land. Rise!" His blessing, followed by cheers as the crowd erupted with great joy, and Mary stood. The people celebrated, cheering, "Mary of Magdala! Blessed of God! Glory to God!" and many turned to the Lord.

Maintaining her healing and freedom from demons by her steady, faithful and sincere relationship with the Lord, boldness increased in Mary's heart the more she shared about Jesus. The region turned to the Lord through the ministry of *Mary of Magdala* and those with her. Lazarus and Martha preached, teaching many about the life and love of Jesus. Mary helped lead the way. Amid conflict and controversy, the vigilant, *dedicated* saints pressed on for months until moving North leaving Lazarus to become the 1st Bishop of Massilia. Martha would travel Northwest with others to Tarascon. Maximin would go to Aix, twenty miles North of Massilia. Soon joined with Sidonius, Mary would work shoulder-to-shoulder with a converted persecutor of believers in Jesus as they made their way to Rome.

NEAR 57 A.D. – ROME

A daring woman of fierce perseverance, the mission-minded-Mary traveled far past her native borders setting off to preach throughout Rome's pagan territories. Through great persecution, suffered by them all, she proclaimed to the people about Christ and His teaching. When many did not believe that He had risen from the dead, showing Himself for 40 days afterward and ascending before their eyes, she repeated to them all she had said to the Apostles on the morning of His Resurrection, preaching, *"I have seen the Lord!"* recounting all His words.

Mary remained with the women of the established house churches in Rome. For two years after Paul's departure and first court judgment (58 A.D.), she failed not, nor grew weary in the diligent serving of God's people. Paul went further as to share his appreciation of her in his preaching, mentioning her to the believers in Rome saying, "Greet Mary, who has done much for us."

Quickly becoming her message and with fiery accuracy, she continued to articulate the whole of His Passion to the lost. Many converted and added to their number, but not without persecution, fierce resistance or challenge. None of this deterred the laborers.

Persecution continued to increase against God's people amid sharp critique and threat of death. "None of these gods you pray to shed blood for you, for your sins to be wiped away. Can any of your gods answer why? Jesus said..." Mary exhorted with boldness until interrupted by a doubter.

"You speak of the prophet. He was just a man! You?" his callous face twisted, *"just* a woman. By what authority do you speak, *Jew?"* came the sharp words of a doubtful, angry Greek in the crowd.

Mary, hearing his words, turned to see him face to face, "By God's authority and in His Name, Jesus. I am *more* than a woman, *more* than my faith! I am of God's own elect, baptized in His Spirit, full of His fire. You!" she stepped toward the doubter, cautiously, "He died for, *shedding His own blood for,* that *you* may have what we speak of. Will you turn from your wicked ways?" she asked, his doubt riddled face. Many people agreed with Mary and turned to hear more.

The Greek man who doubted, considered her words but turned away, disappearing into the overcrowded market.

With this anointing, Mary made her rounds preaching throughout the region. Engaging all who drew near to listen or inquire, saving multitudes for the Lord. She preached alongside the Apostles who greatly cared for her. Holding her in loving esteem, their unity of bonding peace created an atmosphere where God's presence could be felt, tangibly. An atmosphere for miracles, signs and wonders. An atmosphere that honored God.

Soon, word would arrive to them all; one by one they would learn of the fierce evil intent on silencing the witnesses of Jesus even further. Andrew suffered a scourging death for days. He was the next of them to fall.

THE GREAT FIRE OF ROME

Fierce anger blazed against the hated followers of Jesus when the Great Fire erupted. Rome was ablaze. Six days of devastation consumed the Empire. So complete and far-reaching, with Rome's Caesar, Nero thought of as the arsonist. Rumored accusations fueled the fire that scorched everything in its path, being blamed on the Christians; on all who believed in Jesus. The most horrific assault against believers, in the history of the world, was unleashed. The spirit of anti-Christ could hide his face no more.

James the Less fell to the dust, barely alive, hurled from the high wall of the Temple, to an angry mob who stoned and clubbed him to death. The name of Jesus on his lips, the son of Cleophas outlived all the early disciples, except John. James' unflinching testimony of Jesus led to his death. He refused to deny Jesus.

Paul, once the Chief Persecutor of the church, was beheading outside the walls of Rome (64 A.D.) Peter also was slain. Hanging upside down, the disfigured, crucified Peter moaned a blood curdled,

"Forgive me, forgive me, forgive me..." Buzzards circled the dead, red-stained land, strewn with bodies too many to number.

Within a few short years, Galilee was sieged by Romans under Titus. In a disastrous Sea battle of devilish proportions, Vespasian ruled over her ports and shores, plunging the region to ruin as far as Magdala.

Despite their fierce might and the valiant efforts of Josephus leading, tens of thousands would lose their lives trying to defend their stand on Magdala's shores. The rest, *enslaved,* if they were strong enough. The slaughter so great, from the bloody Lake Gennesaret to the once beautiful Sea of Galilee, now full of dead bodies. None escaped the sword that day.

The beautiful Magdala was dead.[8]

THE SCROLLS

John outlived them all. Seventy years had passed since the Resurrection of Jesus. John suffered greatly surviving being boiled in oil. A Son of Thunder, John lived the last of his life exiled to the Island of Patmos. It was the cave of the Apocalypse, which translates to *my killing.*

Alone with the light at the end of his days, John scribed the scrolls of the Book of Revelation, closing his eyes. He had seen *so much.*

"The beautiful Mary of Magdala, *tossed* by the storms of life," came an old familiar voice continuing to share the story of Mary, "chose to learn at the feet of her Lord, absorbing His words," she strained. "Pressing to hear His voice, Mary passionately drank in each

---

[8] Josephus Flavius (Wars 3, Chapter 10). Magdala (Greek) Taricheae, is the place where Jews attempted to make a stand against Vespasians troops. (Masada pg. 63 by Tim McNeese © 2003

lesson, nourishing her ravaged soul. She loved Him *dearly,* devotedly anointing Him. In humble, worshipful adoration and respect, Mary honored His sacrificial life, refusing to be stopped by her enemies." Sarah sat leaning on her cushioned stump stool, nestling Martha's doll on her lap. She continued to share the story of Mary, *the Magdalene.*

"Mary stood near the cross as Jesus died," eyeing the gathered group of children that filled the room, lovingly, "her eyes were fixed on the love of Jesus. It was etched on His bruised, bloody body," she wept. "Mary worshipfully prepared ointment for His corpse, refusing to leave when others ran to hide. *It was Mary* whom the Lord chose *to appear to* when He rose, blessing her to preach His ascension for the rest of her days."

"I was just her *servant-girl* then," wept Sarah. The children sat silent, watching her tears flow down her cheek, wetting the broken alabaster piece. "It was I who was attacked by the Great Lake that day," she smiled, wiping her tears. Turning to the roomful of children that gathered, she whispered, "Mary helped me forgive. We were forced to leave our homeland, forced to flee the persecution. Forced to flee from hate."

A young girl leaned forward to ask, "Were you afraid, grandmother?"

Sarah, taking the broken piece of alabaster in her hand and wiping it dry, turned grievously, "Oh, yes! Very afraid. We were alone in the world."

MARY'S CAVE

Mary moved through her home, a *dim-lit* cave, to a table of items spread out near her bed cushions. Neatly beside her dried bundle of myrrh and cracked vessel of oil, lay her mother's pin and Martha's doll, slightly dusty. Closing her eyes, she picked up the pin and kissed it, raising it to her hair.

A cascading scroll of images, imprinted on her heart, flowed through her memories as Mary, aged and full of days, remembered Jesus. His beautiful face. The sound of His voice filling her. The look of His eyes through her soul. The way He loved the people. She picked up Martha's doll.

Near the entrance of the cave Mary heard the subtle brush of angel's wings and noticed the fragrance in the cave changed. It had been so long ago, yet she could still smell the fragrance of His love. "Jesus," she whispered. "I love You so much. I miss You so much," she said aloud, just under her breath, remembering His beautiful smile. Mary cried.

Rapturous vibrations of angelic melody filled her senses as Mary first recalled seeing Jesus, still a stained sinner, with nothing but a fading hope for love. Her life was forever changed once He touched her. Nestling the broken fragment of alabaster to her bosom, held by a thin red cord, Mary reached for her heart, "When He died, I died," she's always known. "When He rose from death to new life, *so did I*, in Him. My faith tells me so," she settled within herself.

Closing her eyes, the breeze whispered over her body. Mary clasped the beautiful alabaster that still lay at her heart, tightly. She stood at the foot of her cave listening for the sound of her Lord, as if she expected to hear Him. Alone in the place God carved out for her, her long hair cascaded a glistening radiance of what had now become a somewhat silver/white crowning cover. The length of it draped her, blowing slightly in the wind. A peaceful smile on her face, Mary, beautifully poised as if to be lifted aged gracefully, living for God.

Taking a deep breath, a curious smile broke forth. Her thoughts turned heavenward, as the eyes of her heart looked for Him, Whom her soul loved.

She always held more in her heart than she let anyone know. So many beautiful lessons the Lord taught her eager mind and heart. Mary had loved and *been* loved. She knew it *very* well.

Her life of sinful indulgence and vain pride ultimately led to the loss of her reputation. The Lord never disputed the multiple accusations made against Mary, but instead, sharply defended her. Jesus completely forgave the woman of all her sins and healed her life, making her whole. Jesus became her Deliverance.

Alone in the cave, Mary made her way down the overgrown path, vividly recalling the horrors of the persecution of believers. Still able to hear the screams of slaughtered, *innocent*, multitudes of people. Mary remembered Josiah. She fondly recalled Peter, Paul and James and their stalwart stands for faith and devoted love of Jesus. She remembered Thomas' doubt and Levi's weeping at the glory of God, closing her eyes again. How she missed Martha, lovingly squeezing her doll.

The lust of the eyes, the lust of the flesh and the pride of life all lost Mary when she gave herself fully to the Lord Jesus that day. Mary Magdalene was forever changed.

A faint smile on her face, her thoughts embraced the memories of John and Mary, Mother of our Lord, and how He raised her brother from the dead.

"I AM the Bread of Life," His voice echoed through her soul, again. Mary could only press on as His words ran through her *as soft as the breeze.*

"I'm so hungry, Lord," she whispered, clasping the alabaster piece. Descending through the peaceful tree lined woody path, frail and fragile but determined, she knew she must make it to Maximin at the chapel, before the sun set. The rays from the sun barely lit through the trees of the path she must take. Mary moved on.

The voice of the Lord grew louder within her with each step. *"Where are your accusers? Has no one condemned you?"* she could still hear His sweet voice asking that day.

"No one, Lord" she smiled, whispering softly, as if He stood right next to her.

Maximin, now Bishop, prompted by the Holy Spirit, quickly made his way to the faintly beaten path through the thick woods, toward her cave. Nearing the ascent of the mountain and upon seeing Mary, he rushed to embrace her tightly and lovingly, feeling her weakness. Mary was dying. "Woman of God, you've done well," smiled Maximin, noticing her frailty.

"I miss Him so much, Maximin. I miss His voice, His face," she wept laying her head on his chest, her breathing labored and faint.

Taking a broken piece of bread, once more Maximin ministered communion to the weak servant, and gave her to drink of the cup.

"Bishop of Aix; mighty man of God..." Mary whispered dryly. "Thank you for caring for me. Thank you for showing me love and kindness," wept the dying saint, losing her balance and growing very weak.

Dropping the portions that remained to catch the dying saint, he lifted her gently toward himself, holding her firmly to his chest, the doll falling to the ground. A light, soft drizzle sprinkled softly on the faded face of her.

His mission now ending, Maximin carried the weak and dying Mary of Magdala through the woods toward the place of their worship. He approached the chapel door, the sun setting behind him, at last.

Sarah lit a small lamp near the altar of the old chapel, when the door opened abruptly. Gasping, Sarah turned to see it was Mary, and a grief struck Maximin, and stood, breathless, her eyes welling tearfully.

Maximin entered slowly, walking the aged aisle of the old chapel laying Mary down gently at the altar, the alabaster piece at her breast.

Sarah rushed to her, throwing herself over Mary's dying body, and wept.

Our hearts are restless
until they rest in Thee, Lord!

St. Augustine

Mary died at the age of 72,
full of life and love.

A simple woman who loved Jesus,
appreciating Him her whole life. She was so
grateful to Him as He was of her, as through
His *own* lips it was said of her:

"Truly I tell you wherever this Gospel is preached
in *all the world*, what she has done will also be
told in memory of her." ~ Jesus

Mary Magdalene
lived out her life according to history,
in the cave called La Sainte-Baume in France, where she is said
to have been ministered communion daily,
by the Angels of the Lord.

It is further believed that angels miraculously transported
her from the cave by Marseille, La Sainte-Baume, to Aix and into
St. Maximin, where she received the last sacraments before dying.

No longer obscure, no longer silent, Mary Magdalene's story
continues to stir debate. While some would *stone her still*, she is held
in the Holy esteem of sainthood by the Catholic, Orthodox, Anglican,
Lutheran churches, and most of the world.

By the fourth century she was declared
'Apostle to the Apostles'
by Orthodox theologian Augustine.

Today she is revered as the woman
whom the Lord made Apostle to the Apostles.

Mary Magdalene's passion for righteousness,
justice and above all love, continues to
burn in and work through the hearts of a host
of men and women today.

Like Mary, our only strength, our only hope
to *know* love has been found at the feet of
Jesus Christ.

"Young Magdalene"

THE END

The murderous persecution of Christians intensifies worldwide, to this day. The blood of the martyrs cries out, 'Come *quickly*, Lord Jesus.'

For, if you confess with your mouth 'Jesus is Lord' and believe in your heart, God raised Him from the dead, you shall be saved. *Romans 10:9*

Amen.

FROM THE AUTHOR

The story of Mary Magdalene has, for centuries, filled the minds and hearts of all who love the Lord with wondrous curiosity. Who was she and why did she *fully and devotedly* live for Jesus? What was so different about *this* Mary?

By taking liberties at *poetic license and creative expression,* in my attempt to connect the dots, I chose to include the *vein of legend* that spoke of Mary Magdalene's potential encounters: one, with Emperor Tiberius. Some may decide this portion to be an exaggeration of truth and perhaps, to a degree, they are correct. In tracking her legend, though, I settled to include it toward the end of her journey. My hope was to dispel the lore of Easter as *pagan,* instead giving the glory of that marked holiday *back* to the Lord. By choosing to restore the familiar tradition to a more Christ centered symbolism of new life, in the *use* of an egg, it was Augustine who first used a chick, emerging from an egg to tell the story of Jesus's Resurrection.

Making for a wonderful addition to an *already beautiful story,* the inclusion of Tiberius is an interesting one. Readers can research *on their own, and decide for themselves,* if it could have happened. *Could He, Who turned the Nile red have done the same with an egg?* Tradition also continues, that after landing in Rha, Mary and the others converted the people of Masillia of *their idolatry and paganism. Many miracles occurred through her ministry, evangelizing the region.*

Regarding the life of *Mary of Magdala,* some scenes were depicted *outside* of known Scriptural accounts. In portions of the story that lend to the dramatization of her youth, for example, I hoped to create a sense of what Mary, as a child prior to her encounter with Jesus, may have been like, while Joseph fled with Jesus to Egypt. The culture of her day and other historic accounts were included in my research of those days, throughout the story.

Ultimately, I hoped to help bring honor to the only woman in the Gospels *other than* His Mother Mary, to have shared such a close relationship with the Lord Jesus Christ, as shown in the Scripture.

With adequate leads to her *presence and work* in Rome and abroad, I included Paul's greeting in the Book of Romans, (57 A.D.) to the believers in Rome, *"greet Mary, who has worked much for us."* I believe it lends to more reason that she did not remain in St. Baume *exclusively,* as believed by many. It is my opinion, that it was *well within her capacity and ability* to journey *to and from* Rome and *anywhere* else, *prompted of the Holy Spirit,* retreating to St. Baume, Aix as Jesus did to the House in Bethany after His journeys and ministry travels.

Is *anything* too hard for the Lord? Could it be possible that she preached, reaching and converting many after all she witnessed? So much more happened after she landed safely on the shores of France. Why would she have stopped witnessing about Jesus and stay exclusively in a cave?

> God's Word says, *"You are the light of the world. A city on a hill cannot be hidden. Neither do people light a lamp and put it under a basket. Instead, they set it on a lampstand and it gives light to everyone in the house."* Matthew 5:15

> *Later as they were eating, Jesus appeared to the eleven and rebuked them for their unbelief and hardness of heart, because they did not believe those who had seen Him after He had risen. And He said to them,*

> *'Go into all the world and preach the Gospel to every creature. Whoever believes and is baptized will be saved, but whoever does not believe will be condemned.'* Mark 16:15

ABOUT THE AUTHOR

Sandra Cerda developed a love for creative writing in elementary school in San Antonio, Tx. Re-capturing the beauty and art of journaling during a very dark and difficult time in her personal life and ministry, she catapulted her career by authoring and publishing four books in one year and founded New Life Publishing, a subsidiary to her non-profit charity/church organization. After recuperating in 2013, she preached her first public speaking engagement. In one year, she founded and launched the Gathering of Warriors *Prophetic-Spiritual Warfare* Crusades and emerged to write her 1st novel and screenplay on Mary Magdalene *by 2016*. In less than two years her work on the life of the *Apostle to Apostles* developed for film and worldwide influence in ministering the redemptive love of Jesus Christ for the lost.

Author and publisher, Sandra Cerda, was ordained as Minister of the Gospel by the laying on of hands through the late John Osteen, Lakewood Church in Houston, in the early 1990s.

Sandra Cerda is the Founding Pastor of New Life Ministries in Texas. Her strengths are prophetic spiritual warfare and the five-fold ministry anointing. Sandra Cerda is the Creative Visionary and Executive Producer for Mary Magdalene and The Mary Magdalene Project.

For more on this book/film and study-guide project and to subscribe for E-Letter updates please visit the websites at www.MaryMagdalene.Film and at www.SandraCerda.com

Sandra resides near the city of Houston, Texas USA with her large and growing family and her *warrior husband* of 30+ years!

REFERENCES:

Magdala.Org, The Magdalena Institute, TheNazareneWay.Com, OrthoDoxWiki.Org, CatholicCompany.com, Antiochian.Org, Quora.Com, Beliefnet.Com/BenWitherington EWTN.Com/Relics Of Mary Magdalene, AmazingBibleTimeline.Com, JohnPratt.com, SmithsonianMag.Com, Mary College Library – Oxford University, The Coming Of The Saints By John W. Tyler, MaryPublishing.Org, The Legend Of Mary Magdalene, Oca.Org(OrthadoxChurchOfAmerica), Bible.Org, HomePages.Neiu.Edu, BlackHistoryInTheBible.Com, AllAboutReligion.Org, The Life Of Mary Magdalene from the *Legenda Aurea* (13thCentury) by Jacopodi Voragine, Life of Mary Magdalene by Rabanus Maurus (Archbishop of Mayence – 770-856 A.D., The Life of Christ in Stereo by Johnston M. Cheney, C.H. Spurgeon on Mary Magdalene 1868, Mary Magdalene: The Golden Legend, The Quest for Mary Magdalene: History & Legend by Michael Hagg, Mary Magdalene: Relics in France, University of Rochester, Department.Kings.Edu, BiblicalArcheology.Org, BibleHub, ChristianExaminer.Com, BibleArcheology.Org, ChristianExaminer.Com, ShamelessPoppery.com, Remnant Newspaper, The Jerusalem Post, Christian Courier, StudyLight.Org, BibleJourney.Org, TheseStoneWalls.com, Levitt.com, TheWayPrepared.Com, SeeTheHolyLand.net, RestlessPilgrim.net, KingdomWarrior.com/LepersAnointing, Hendrik Wieland/3 Separate Anointings, geni.com/people/Cyrus-of-Magdala-King-of-the-Benjamite-Tribe geni.com/people/St-Mary-Mary, On Judas/Simon: JohnsonNewTestament commentary vol iii, John/Feeding Upon Christ, McGarvey/thefour-foldgospel/xii after prayer JesusSelects/barton/hislastweek/thursdaythedayofFellowship, www.ucg.org/bible-study-tools/bible-questions-and-answers/what-happened-to-the-resurrected-saints-mentioned-in, globalchristiancenter.com/christian-living/lesser-known-bible-people/31288-simons-son-judas, Augustine/homiliesonthegospelofjohn/tractate iv john chapterxiii, Acquinas/summatheological/whetherchristgavehisbody, WhatChristiansWantToKnow/how-did-the-12-apostles-die britannica.com/biography/Pontius-Pilate, www.bibleodyssey.org/en/people/main-articles/herod-the-great, www.bible.org/seriespage/24-when-division-becomes-multiplication-acts-153-1610, biblebelievers.org.au/moongod, http://www.ukapologetics.net/11/judascommunion.htm en.wikipedia.org/wiki/2015KidnappingAndBeheadingOfCoptsInLibya and christian-history.org/gospel-of-mary-Mary...www.bible.ca/synagogues/Magdala-Taracheae-Migdal-bible-ancient-synagogues-first-century-oldest-pre70AD-Jesus-archeology-top-plan-Mary-Magdelene-heart-table-4-freestanding-columns-50bc.htm...Works of Flavius Josephus: Sacred Texts, Wars of the Jews: Josephus www.bible-history.com/geography/ancient-israel/magdala.html www.monasteryicons.com/product/story-of-the-first-easter-egg/did-you-know *and* www.melbournecatholic.org.au/Melbourne-News/did-mary-magdalene-invent-the-easter-egg, www.monasteryicons.com and melbournecatholic.org.au/Tiberius, Jesus-Lazarus-Messiah-Robert-Powell on Amazon, Mary Magdalene: Insights From Ancient Magdala, by Jennifer Ristine

And the inspired Word of God.

CONTACT & RESOURCES

Available for Public Speaking & Ministry.
Mary Magdalene Art & Products can be found at
www.SandraCerda.com and Facebook @SandraCerda,
@MaryMagdalene.Film and @MaryMagdaleneProducts
See **www.MaryMagdalene.Film** for

More on The Mary Magdalene Project & Subscribe to receive
the Mary Magdalene Newsletter for Updates!

Email: **TheMaryMagdaleneProject@gmail.com**

For more on Sandra Cerda, visit the website at
www.SandraCerda.com
Watch for the Movie: Mary Magdalene
Find Us on IMDb/MaryMagdalene

Bulk Orders available for
Mary Magdalene: *A Historic Novel*,
Mary Magdalene Study-Guide, and
The Oil: *Making Mary Magdalene*

Inquire to: TheMaryMagdaleneProject@gmail.com

More Titles at Amazon/Books/SandraCerda

Water Me, *Lord!* *(Women's Devotional)*

INCEST: The Curse of Destruction...*Reversed!*
(Autobiography) and En Español)

Spiritual Warfare: *The Fight, The Freedom, The Fire*
(A Manual)

Dream Peace: *When God Speaks*
(Bible-Based Dream Interpretation)

On YouTube and FaceBook @ SandraCerda

In dedication to her mother and daughters, **The Mary Magdalene Collection** by *Sandra Cerda* is growing! New items are rich in 1st century influence, ingredients and wares, including our line of Therapeutic *Natural/Organic* Soaps & Products; a growing line of items sure to enhance the appearance and glow of your skin!

In addition to the book, Mary Magdalene: *A Historic Novel,* **The Mary Magdalene Study-Guide** covers the in-depth research of the entire story and points of interest. Complete with References, Footnotes and plenty of writing space.

The Oil: *Making Mary Magdalene* gives the behind-the-scenes story of the Author's journey from conception to production, in creating the story of Mary Magdalene. The Author shares of the multiple tragedies of lost loved-ones, life-threatening heartbreaks, and moments of *great* isolation as well as *huge* breakthroughs, the faith-walk through the Valley-of-Decision, the Valley-of-Ono and the Valley of the *Shadow of Death*. From Texas, New York, Los Angeles, Idyllwild and Houston, the Author's journey to *"hear from God"* for this story is riveting!

A portion from the Mary Magdalene Collection is donated to the Antonio L. Santos Memorial Fund in memory of Sandra's father, who passed before learning of this work. For more on his legacy and this mission, his military contribution, and growing gallery, see www.SandraCerda.Com/TonySantosMemorial

The Mary Magdalene Study-Guide
Accompaniment to the Novel

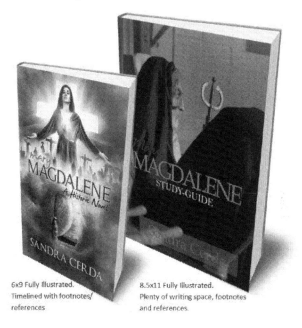

6x9 Fully Illustrated.
Timelined with footnotes/
references

8.5x11 Fully Illustrated.
Plenty of writing space, footnotes
and references.

Study-Guide is $8^{1/2}$ x 11, Fully Illustrated with plenty of writing space.
Includes footnotes and reference links.

Study

- The Law of Stoning
- The Feedings (there were three)
- The Anointings (there were three)
- The Persecution of the Martyrs and Today
- What were her demons?
- The Appearances of Jesus
- The Great Commission
- The France/Rome debate
- The Upper Room: *She was there!*

And so much more!

Available on Amazon and in E-Reader Digital format for all devices.

Sheri Powell's **Pausing With God and Woman of Excellence** *selections will engage, encourage, empower you to make the most of every season of your life!*

A Woman of Excellence: *The Ministry of My Mother A Memoir* $9.95
Shares how the dynamics of a mother and daughter relationship may range from healthy to unwholesome. This relationship can affect you on so many levels: emotionally, mentally, physically, financially, and spiritually. *The Ministry of My Mother* will remind some and refresh others to:
• Remember, it's not how you started, but how you finish.
• Realize that we all experience a storm or two at some point in our lives.
• Reexamine our relationship with our mother, our daughter, but most of all with ourselves.

Pausing With God A Journey Through Menopause *(English and Spanish)* $12.95
Connects the dots from puberty to menstruation to a season of menopause. Menopause is a natural and inevitable time in a woman's life, but just the anticipation of this event can have one on pins and needles. From hot flashes to weight gain, every woman will experience different symptoms and to various degrees. Instead of focusing on what we can't do, we'll benefit most by setting our mind on what we can do.

Pausing In His Presence: *A Shut-In Experience* $12.95
A sequel to Pausing with God: A Journey through Menopause, Sheri reveals the importance of making Pausing With God a lifestyle. She communicates in a simplistic manner that no matter what season of life we find ourselves, when we take the time to pause in His presence, we will discover peace that passes all understanding.

Available at PausingWithGod.com | Amazon | Barnes & Noble | Books-A-Million

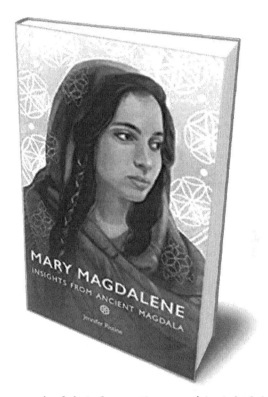

For a wonderful, informative, and insightful
book on the *life and legacy* of
Mary Magdalene and Ancient Magdala,
read Jennifer Ristines'

Mary Magdalene:
Insights From Ancient Magdala

Available on Amazon.

Visit Magdala.Org/The Magdalena Institute

Visit **www.SandraCerda.com** for a full line of *Art & Products* from the Mary Magdalene Collection!

The Mary Magdalene **Online E-Store** allows you to order beautiful pencil sketched illustrations included within the story, along with many other great gift items. Downloadable Art and **Print on Demand** mugs, jewelry, T-shirts, canvas bags and more make unique and *wonderful conversation starters and gifts.*

Share the beautiful story of Christ's redemptive love as demonstrated through the life of the *Apostle to Apostles.*

More at www.MaryMagdalene.Film and on Facebook @MaryMagdaleneProducts and @MaryMagdaleneMovie

Titles Published by

Sandra Cerda & New Life Publishing

Available On Amazon

Cacophony: *A Tale of Faith & Fear*

by Jacob Airey, Southern California

Unity: *On Earth As It Is In Heaven*

by Dan Almeter, Augusta, Georgia

Allelujia! *The Return of the Protype*

by Don Swenson, PhD., *(Prof. Emeritus)*

Mount Royale University, Calgary, Alberta, Canada

No Coincidences

by Bobby Lopez, San Antonio, Texas

Spiritual Strategies for the Hood

by Apostle Timothy Rambo - Auburn, Washington

New Life Publishing

Bringing *1st Time Authors* to Print!

On Facebook @ *1st Time Authors*

186

Made in the USA
Columbia, SC
10 September 2020

19680824R00111